Family Walks
in the
Lake District

Barry McKay

HIGH INTEREST · LOW MILEAGE

Scarthin Books of Cromford
Derbyshire
1993

Family Walks in the Lake District

General Editor: Norman Taylor

The Country Code

Respect the life and work of the countryside
Guard against all risk of fire
Fasten all gates
Keep your dogs under close control
Keep to the public paths across farmland
Use gates or stiles to cross fences, hedges and walls
Leave livestock, crops and machinery alone
Take all your litter home
Help to keep all water clean
Protect wildlife, plants and trees
Take care on country roads
Make no unnecessary noise

Walking the routes in this book

All the routes in this book have been walked, in most cases, several times prior to publication and we have taken great care to ensure that they are on rights of way. However, changes occur all the time in the landscape; should you meet any obstructions, please let us know. Serious obstructions can be brought to the attention of the local branch of the Ramblers Association and the Rights of Way section of the County Council.

Published by Scarthin Books of Cromford, Derbyshire 1993

Printed in Great Britain at The Alden Press, Oxford

ISBN 0907758 401

Cover illustration by Andrew Ravenwood: Wasdale Head (route 16)

Waterfall on Black Beck (route 8).

Dedication

For Sarah and Becky

Preface

When our children were small we wanted to share with them our love of the mountains and valleys of Cumbria and the best way to do this was, we felt, by continuing a life-long pastime of walking there. We failed to realise that once they were past being back-packed around the high fells those same heights would be beyond them for several years. We then discovered the delights of the lowland areas. We also discovered that car parks, toilets, and places which sold ice cream had a greater importance than previously thought possible.

We thought then that this was the sort of guide book that was needed. A few years later Scarthin Books approached us to add a Lake District volume to their growing *Family Walks* series. We little realised how much time and effort it would require.

All these walks have been undertaken by our daughters, Sarah and Becky, when between the ages of four and thirteen. Their opinions have in many ways influenced the final selection. A number of friends have also walked the routes and, not infrequently, pointed out our errors. To Polly Atterbury, Anne, Tony, Daniel and Amy Martin, Barbara and Matthew Cunningham, Julian and Anne Roberts, Helen Wadlington, George Zacharewicz, Julian Brooks, Lucy Sturton, Patrick, Marion, Rebecca and James Leach we are indebeted. We are also grateful to David Atkinson, Tom Newton, Mike Shuttleworth and Chris Wilson for reading the texts and offering advice and suggestions.

Cumbria is a majestically beautiful county of changing moods and moments. Too many people see only the view through the windscreen of their cars. The only way to thoroughly enjoy and appreciate the fells and valleys is on foot. We have often done so and continue to do so. Our hope is that, through this book, we can share some of our pleasure.

Barry McKay
Appleby-in-Westmorland, New Year's Day 1993

Contents

Map of the area

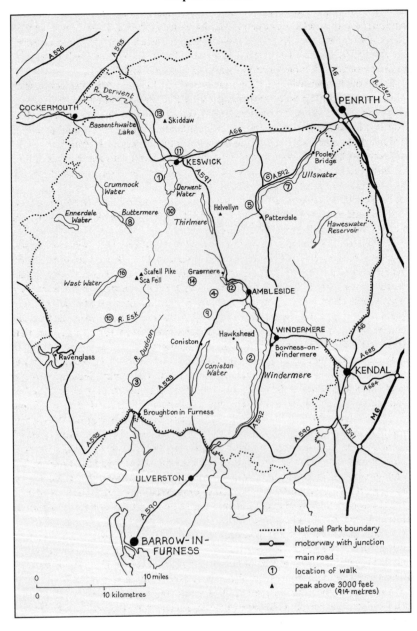

Legend:
- .... National Park boundary
- —o— motorway with junction
- —— main road
- ① location of walk
- ▲ peak above 3000 feet (914 metres)

Introduction

For some two hundred years the 'mountains, lakes, valleys, woods, waters and meadows' of the Lake District have held a peculiar fascination for countless thousands of visitors. Geology, land-forming processes, particularly glaciation, and the agricultural and industrial activities of man have combined to create a landscape of considerable variation within a relatively small area.

Many of the men who went on to climb in the Alps and Himalayas learnt or polished their peculiar skills on the crags in which Cumbria abounds. The scope of this present work, however, does not seek to offer advice to the tyro rock-climber. Instead it has a more modest end, a simple introduction suitable for all ages, but particularly families, to some of the most beautiful scenery of England.

All the walks in this book have been tested by children between the ages of four and thirteen. Several of the walks are aimed at the younger ages whilst others are more suitable for older children. A scale of difficulty can be found elsewhere in the book. We have tried to select walks which take in as many aspects of the area as possible and have included both gentle lowland walks as well as more testing routes in the higher fells suitable for older children.

A good compass and the knowledge to use it are worthwhile. As an introduction to its use *The Spur Book of the Map and Compass* by Terry Brown & Rob Hunter, Frederick Warne, 1987, takes some beating. A whistle should be carried, in an easily accessible place, at all times. The distress signal for the mountain rescue is six long blasts repeated at minute intervals. Please remember that people die on these mountains every year so take care. Use your judgment as to what your children can manage and remember that good judgment comes from experience and that experience is frequently gained through bad judgment.

Walking in England is always fraught with the problem of weather, this is perhaps more true of Cumbria than anywhere else in the country. Notice boards in many areas and Tourist Information Offices in the fells display daily weather forecasts. Weather forecasts and fell conditions are always available by telephone on Windermere (05394) 45151. It is quite possible for the weather to change dramatically, and potentially dangerously, within minutes. It is therefore essential that all members of the party be correctly equipped. Good waterproofs are essential and walking boots are strongly advised, certainly on the more mountainous walks. A number of walking and climbing equipment shops in the area rent boots by the day or week or sell secondhand children's boots. Wellington boots are not always suitable. Quite apart from being uncomfortable on rock they, and trainers, can be downright dangerous when descending.

A change of clothing for younger children is advisable and remember that several thin sweaters provide more warmth than one thick one. A hat is wise, as not only is the head a major source of heat loss but the wind, particularly in exposed areas, can cause painful earache. We always carry a bivouac bag. This is a large polythene bag which can be used as shelter in case of injury and also provides a clean and dry place to sit while sandwiches are eaten. A very good, and reasonably priced one is produced by the Scout Association and sold through their shops.

Footpaths are frequently well marked and stiles abound throughout the area. Indeed for walkers Cumbria is very well appointed with routes and other aids to enjoyable days. These paths, the cairns (small piles of stones) that frequently mark them and the stiles that ease the way along are maintained by a loyal body of, frequently volunteer, workers. Respect their time and effort.

Follow the Country Code and particularly keep dogs on leads. The living of a hill farmer is precarious enough without a portion of his meagre profits being killed by badly controlled dogs which, to quote the owners of several, "are only playing."

Choosing a walk

Allow plenty of time to complete the walk in daylight. At least one hour should be allowed for every two miles and a further hour for every 1500 feet of ascent. If the party contains small children one mile an hour will be more realistic. Plenty of time should be included for stops. If the fells are shrouded in mist stay off them and stick to the valleys.

Paths

Many of the paths in the Lake District are public rights of way. In the fells the path is frequently marked by cairns which can also aid your descent if you are caught out by bad weather or poor visibility. In most cases the paths are well worn but there are occasional exceptions where we suggest less frequented routes.

Maps

We hope that the maps in this book, used in conjunction with the route descriptions will suffice in most instances. However, you are strongly advised to carry the Ordnance Survey Outdoor Leisure map of the area in which you are walking.

Refreshments

You will readily appreciate that parts of the Lake District are very sparsely populated. In some of the more remote areas easy access to refreshments can be difficult and opening times can vary with the seasons. Where none are readily available in the course of, or at the end of a walk we have suggested nearby towns and villages. Most pubs in the area welcome children. Catering times vary but in general it is unwise to expect food after about 1.30 pm.

Public Transport

Public transport to the more remote areas can be infrequent or even non-existent; however a list of transport operators, applicable to the walks, can be found at the end of the book. Contact them for advice. Water travel is also possible and can add to the delights of a day out. Steamers cover Windermere and Ullswater and there is a lake launch on Derwent. For times of sailings check with the operating companies whose telephone numbers are given at the end of the book.

All the walks in this book start from, or close to, recognised car parks or accepted parking areas. The small lay-bys on narrow roads carrying signs stating them to be "Passing Places" are exactly that. They are not parking places.

Finally, enjoy yourselves and watch where you put your feet.

Windermere Ferry (route 2).

9

THOMAS ARTHUR LEONARD
FOUNDER OF CO-OPERATIVE AND COMMUNAL HOLIDAYS
AND 'FATHER' OF THE OPEN-AIR MOVEMENT IN THIS COUNTRY
BORN LONDON MARCH 12th 1864.
DIED CONWAY JULY 19th 1948.
BELIEVING THAT 'THE BEST THINGS ANY MORTAL HATH
ARE THOSE WHICH EVERY MORTAL SHARES' HE ENDEAVOURED
TO PROMOTE 'JOY IN WIDEST COMMONALTY SPREAD'

Scramble past a memorial slab set in the rock on Cat Bells.

Grading: Moderate with hard ascent

Cat Bells and Brandelhow Park

Outline

Hawes End – Skelgill Bank – Cat Bells – Hause Gate – Brackenburn – Brandelhow Bay – Brandelhow Park – Victoria Bay – Otterbield Bay – Hawes End.

Summary

A varied route which combines open fellside, ridge, woodland and lakeside walking. Fine views across Derwent Water and into the Derwent Fells and Newlands Valley enhance the walk over Cat Bells while the lowland stretch through woodland along the lakeside provides a pleasant contrast. The paths are good and easy to follow throughout. Due to the deserved popularity of Cat Bells, erosion control of the path is in operation. There may be minor variations from the route described below but they will be clearly signposted on the fell.

Attractions

This walk begins at the northern end of a ridge of fells which stretches along the western side of Derwent Water but visits only the first summit, that of Cat Bells which at 1400 feet and given its exposed situation, provides an excellent sense of height. The fell's name, according to some authorities, means den of the wild cat, so-called after the animals which were common in the area until the early 19th century. The climb to the summit is stiff in parts but the ascent is broken by some level stretches which allow for a breather on the way. The view from the summit across Derwent Water to Keswick and its splendid backdrop of Skiddaw is magnificent.

From the summit the walk descends at first before following a ridge route to Hause Gate. From there a steep descent on a wide and clear path eventually brings you down to the lakeside at Brandelhow Bay. The Keswick Launch calls at the landing stage there, and also at Victoria Bay a little way up the lake. It is possible to take the launch from Keswick to reach this walk.

The part of the walk alongside the lake passes through the open woodland of Brandelhow Park which is noteworthy as being the first property in the Lake District to be acquired by the National Trust. There are several good places for picnics or paddling along the lake's shore.

Refreshments

There is a good cafe in the excellent landscaped gardens at Lingholm and numerous others in nearby Keswick.

Route 1

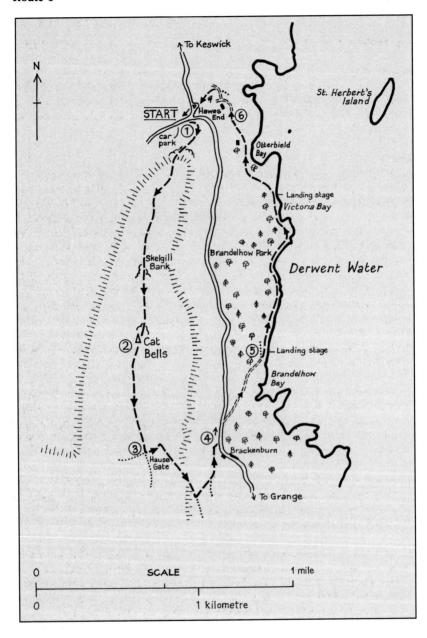

To Keswick

N

St. Herbert's Island

START

Hawes End

car park

① ⑥

Otterbield Bay

Landing stage
Victoria Bay

Brandelhow Park

Skelgill Bank

Derwent Water

② △ Cat Bells

⑤ — Landing stage

Brandelhow Bay

③ Hause Gate

④

Brackenburn

To Grange

0	SCALE	1 mile

0	1 kilometre

Route 1

Cat Bells and Brandelhow Park

4 miles

Start

From the car park (space limited) 150 yards west of the cattle-grid on the road at the base of Cat Bells, 2 miles south of the A66 turning (1 mile west of Keswick) signposted to Portinscale, Lingholm Gardens, Grange and Newlands Valley. OS. Outdoor Leisure, English Lakes NW (GR 247211).

Route

1. *Start up the steps from the north-east corner of the mountain just where the track to the car park leaves the road from Portinscale to Grange. After 100 yards turn left when you meet another path. This will then take you to the summit. The first 800 yards are clearly defined until a rock band is reached in which is set a memorial slab. At the memorial keep to the left and scramble over the rocks for a few yards until the path is once again clearly visible. A further 400 yards will bring you to the hump of Skelgill Bank. The path to the summit can now be seen clearly following the ridge and ascending the final mass of the fell. On the final rock band you might find it more comfortable to scramble straight up the rocks rather than follow the path to the right. It is rather narrow and can give a feeling of considerable exposure. (Besides, scrambling over a few rocks is more fun!)*

2. *The first part of the descent is easily seen from the summit. Continue heading along the ridge with Derwent Water on your left.*

3. *As you descend into the level area at Hause Gate the path down to the left is clearly marked by a length of wooden stake and rail fencing. Follow this path down for about a quarter of a mile to where another path joins on the left. Turn left here and follow this path, which descends diagonally towards a stone wall. Cross the terrace path to reach the wall and follow it through trees to the road.*

4. *At the road turn left and a few yards further on turn right on to a broad track. Continue down the track until a stake and wire fence is seen. Bear right towards a gate in the fence. Go through the gate and keep to the right to come to the edge of the lake and Brandelhow landing stage.*

5. *Keep to the path closest to the lake and follow it through woodland until you reach a gate in a drystone wall at Victoria Bay landing stage. Go through the gate and turn left. The path crosses a field and after 400 yards comes to another gate in a metal stake and rail fence. Go through that gate and cross the field to the next gate, again in a metal stake and rail fence. Go through that gate and turn right on to a drive.*

Continued on page 14

13

6. *Follow the drive past Hawse End house bearing right at the end of the courtyard on to a metalled drive. After 60 yards turn left off the drive and go uphill through a stretch of woodland. A track soon becomes clear and leads you back to the road just below a cattle grid. Turn left on to the road and return to the car park.*

Public Transport

There is no public transport by road but the Keswick Launch serves both Brandelhow and Victoria Bay landing stages.

Keswick launch landing stage at Brandelhow Bay (Skiddaw in the background).

Grading: Easy

Claife Heights from Far Sawrey

Outline
Far Sawrey – Moss Eccles Tarn – Wise Een Tarn – Brown Stone Tarn – High Blind How – Low Pate Crag – Far Sawrey.

Summary
This charming walk takes you through landscape typical of south-eastern Cumbria. The walking is easy with only moderate climbs but parts of the route are boggy so suitable footwear is a must. The first half of the walk is through open country and takes in two very pleasant tarns. The return leg is more demanding, passing through forest with occasional open areas and rocky outcrops. Forestry working in the more heavily wooded areas means the path may vary slightly. Trust the white-painted poles which will mark any changes from the described route.

Attractions
This fine scenic walk takes in the area of high ground which lies between Esthwaite Water and the western shore of Lake Windermere. High ground here however being a relative term when compared with the lofty fells to the north and west, for the highest point of this route is High Blind How at a modest 885 feet. Claife Heights takes its name from the Old Norse *kleif* meaning a steep hill.

The first part of the walk includes Moss Eccles and Wise Een Tarns where there is the added attraction of rocks to scramble over. Thereafter you pass through Forestry Commission plantations which achieve a successful blend of native woodland with imported conifers. Close-planted trees provide a canopy overhead which give you an impression of walking through mysterious wooded tunnels where a juvenile imagination can feast on any number of legendary creatures lurking just out of sight. Boggy clearings, rocky outcrops and other woodland features provide a constantly changing mood to the walk.

The attractions of this walk can be increased by travelling to the start by the ferry across Lake Windermere (2 miles south of Bowness on the A592). Be prepared for a delay at peak times as there is a 10 car maximum, and a further 2¼ miles road walking for foot passengers.

After completing the walk a visit to Hill Top in Near Sawrey is recommended. This was the home of Beatrix Potter, author of the *Tale of Peter Rabbit* and other children's classics and who was much respected as a breeder of local sheep.

Refreshments
Sawrey Hotel serves bar food and admits children. There is also a pub and a tea shop in Near Sawrey.

15

Route 2

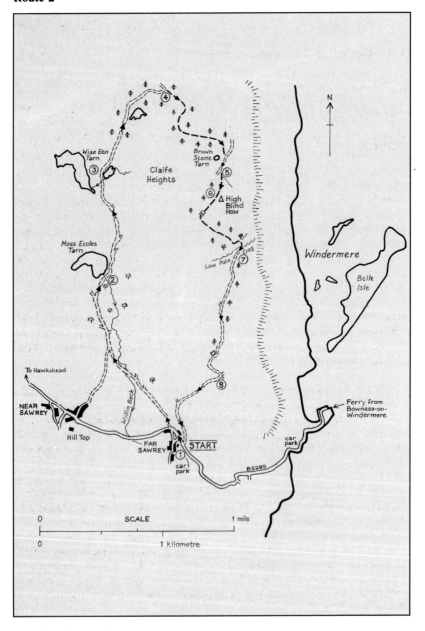

Claife Heights

Wise Een Tarn ③

Windermere

Belle Isle

Brown Stone Tarn ⑤

⑥ △ High Blind How

④

Moss Eccles Tarn ②

Low Pate ⑦ Crag

⑧

To Hawkshead

NEAR SAWREY

Hill Top

FAR SAWREY

START ①

car park

Wilfin Beck

car park

Ferry from Bowness-on-Windermere

B5285

N

SCALE

0 ———————— 1 mile

0 ———————— 1 kilometre

Route 2

Grading: Easy

Claife Heights from Far Sawrey

$5\frac{1}{2}$ miles

Start

The route is described from the car park at the village hall in Far Sawrey (donation requested) opposite the telephone box at the eastern end of the Sawrey Hotel on the B5285, 7 miles south east of Hawkshead. OS Outdoor Leisure, English Lakes SE (GR 379954).

Route

1. *Turn left out of the car park and go along the road towards Near Sawrey. A little way past the Sawrey Hotel take the first right off this road on to Colt House Wray Bridle Path, signposted as a dead end. After 400 yards you cross a cattle grid and shortly afterwards turn left at a signpost to Hawkshead. Continue on that path and cross Wilfin Beck via a narrow footbridge. Shortly afterwards pass through a gate and continue as signposted to Claife Heights along a waymarked path until Moss Eccles Tarn is reached.*

2. *From the tarn the path bears away to the right and slightly uphill. At a fork about 100 yards after you leave the tarn keep to the left. Continue on, keeping left at another (less distinct) fork in the path and passing through a gate, come to Wise Een Tarn with another unnamed and smaller tarn to the right.*

3. *At the far end of the smaller tarn bear to the right towards a plantation ahead. Enter the plantation by the stile at the left corner where a drystone wall meets the boundary fence. Follow a track through the woodland keeping a small tarn (visible through the trees) on your right. The track becomes a broad forestry roadway and starts to descend. After another 200 yards this road turns a sharp left and continues downhill.*

4. *At the apex of this bend there is a painted stake marking a path and a signpost to Hawkshead, Ferry and Sawrey. **Be warned that this signpost can be easily missed.** Follow the signposted path uphill through the woodland following the white-topped stakes and occasional daubs of white paint on trees which denote the route. At a signpost turn right towards Ferry. Watch your step on the tree roots underfoot as they can be very slippery. Continue on across a short stretch of open boggy land and once again ascend into the trees. Follow the natural steps of tree roots and rocks uphill and down until you emerge from the woodland on to a forestry roadway near Brown Stone Tarn.*

Continued on page 18

5. *At the roadway turn right, signposted to Ferry, and after 200 yards turn left by a painted post and re-enter woodland. After another 250 yards, and as you are descending through trees, turn right on to a path which ascends quite steeply and is marked with white-topped stakes. About halfway up this climb there is a path off to the left which takes you out of the woodland and on to the open area around the OS triangulation point at High Blind How.*

6. *Rejoin the main path and continue uphill, go over a footbridge and on until you once again emerge from woodland into a small clearing with a rocky outcrop. Turn sharp left at a signpost to Ferry. Continue downhill, scrambling over the rocks, and re-enter the trees. Carry on through the trees until another signpost is reached, turn left towards Ferry, continue through a rocky outcrop and descend again into woodland. At the next signpost turn right towards Ferry and Sawrey and carry on downhill into a more open area.*

7. *At the bottom of the slope turn right and follow the track with a semi-derelict drystone wall on your left. After about half a mile go through a gate, past a small tarn, and bearing to your left, go downhill between drystone walls until a signpost is reached.*

8. *At the signpost turn right towards Sawrey, pass through a gate and follow the path down into the village. This path meets the road almost directly opposite the car park.*

Public Transport
Ribble Motor Services.

Carved owl on a wall in Broughton Mills.

18

Grading: Moderate

Dunnerdale Fells and Broughton Mills

Outline
River Duddon – Pickthall Ground – High Lickle Bridge – Broughton Mills – Penny Crag Wood – Lumholme – Hovel Knott – River Duddon.

Summary
A very good walk in the southern Dunnerdale Fells which involves a little road walking, though on quiet roads. In general the going is easy apart from a fairly steep climb shortly after the start and a bit of a pull uphill after you leave Broughton Mills. The area is less frequented than other parts of the Lake District and the route is not always easy to follow especially in high summer when bracken can make parts of the path difficult to define.

Attractions
Lying in the south-western corner of the National Park the River Duddon and Dunnerdale Fells are rarely included in the itineraries of most visitors to the district. The area however is well worth visiting and the banks of the River Duddon provide a pleasant place to sit, while children paddle, at the end of the walk.

   The first section takes you up a green lane which served the peat workings on the plateau near Potherilt Hill. After a stretch of more open country the middle section involves a walk through walled farmland by way of Pickthall Ground before a descent into the valley of the River Lickle.

   The descent from Pickthall Ground to the river takes you down an old corpse road variously known as Priest's or Parson's Path or Way (depending on which authority you choose to accept). This is followed by a stretch across farmland to Broughton Mills. There you will find the Blacksmith's Arms, an old beer house dating from 1748, which has good beer, homemade food and excellent ice-cream. It is worth visiting just to see the bar with its large central table surrounded by an old settle. The usual opening hours are 11 to 3 (all day Saturday) and 12 to 2.30 in the winter months. It is closed on Mondays, and on Tuesday and Wednesday lunchtimes from November to March.

   After Broughton Mills there is a short climb through Penny Crag Wood and thereafter fell walking until you reach the road.

Refreshments
As well as the Blacksmith's Arms, there is a cafe in Ulpha and several in Broughton-in-Furness.

Route 3

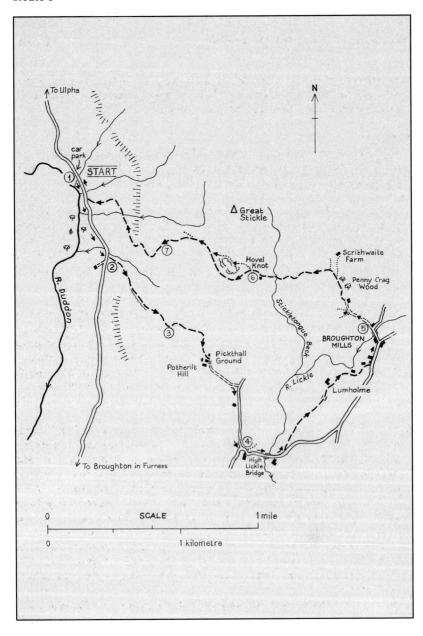

To Ulpha

car park

START ①

N

△ Great Stickle

Scrithwaite Farm

⑦

Hovel Knot

⑥

Penny Crag Wood

R. Duddon

②

③

Stickletongue Beck

⑤

BROUGHTON MILLS

Pickthall Ground

Potherilt Hill

R. Lickle

Lumholme

To Broughton in Furness

④

High Lickle Bridge

SCALE

0   1 mile

0   1 kilometre

Route 3

Grading: Moderate

Dunnerdale Fells and Broughton Mills

6 miles

Start

From a car parking area at an old quarry site alongside the River Duddon south of Ulpha on the Broughton road about 3½ miles north of Broughton-in-Furness. OS Outdoor Leisure, English Lakes SW (GR 199919).

Route

1. *From the car parking area turn left and follow the road for just under half a mile until you reach a path on the left alongside a stream. This is opposite an area signposted for "Turning Only" and just before a private drive.*

2. *Follow the path uphill for several hundred yards. At first you are on the right hand side of a beck which may appear to be dry but after you pass over the crest of the climb cross to the left hand bank. In the far distance there is a drystone wall. Head towards it. Initially you will be walking alongside a drainage cutting but as you come to a bog keep to the left and aim for a gate in the wall a couple of hundred yards ahead.*

3. *Go through the gate and follow a broad path which goes to the left at first before bearing right alongside a drystone wall. Carry on alongside this wall and turn right at a gateway where it meets another wall at right angles. Make for the farmstead about 150 yards ahead and slightly to the left. Go through the yard, turning left to pass in front of the first house, and turn right through the front gate onto a track. Carry on down until you meet a road. Turn right and continue downhill to a road junction.*

4. *At the junction turn left and continue on the road passing between farm buildings and over High Lickle Bridge. Just after the bridge and as the road starts to climb take the footpath, signposted to Broughton Mills, on the left at the end of a length of metal fencing. Cross the first field, keeping to the left of a line of trees. Go over the drystone wall by stone steps and a small gate. Cross the next field to a stone stile in the top right hand corner. Cross this wall and carry on to the hedge boundary. Cross a stile through the hedge and go over a small bridge. Follow the waymark arrows across the field, aiming towards a farm. Go through a wooden gate, turn right and head for a gate in Lumholme farm buildings – a waymark arrow is on the lintel above the gate. Go through the farm and follow the path into Broughton Mills. When you reach the road turn left, pass through the village and over the bridge.*

5. *Where the road turns right at the end of the bridge you take the track straight ahead*

Continued on page 22

signposted to Scrithwaite and Ulpha. The track, which is metalled for a few hundred yards, is between drystone walls and climbs gently uphill. The path bears right in front of a farmhouse, and 100 yards further on, by a white lime-washed building, bears left and climbs more steeply for a short way until a gate is reached at Penny Crag Wood. Go through the gate and bear to the left uphill alongside a drystone wall. After about 250 yards the path forks. Keep to the right and follow the path until you come to a gate near to a barn (note the hogg hole in the wall alongside the barn, which allows sheep to slip from field to field).

6. *Go through the gate and follow the path until it forks. Here you can either follow the right hand path up and over a col or continue around it. These two paths meet again at a junction marked by a small cairn. At the cairn keep to the left and carry on, keeping left at the next fork and with the rising ground on your left and moorland on your right, for about 500 yards.*

7. *The path then descends towards a boulder-strewn pool (occasionally dried up) in front of a narrow rocky ridge. At the left-hand edge of the ridge turn right and go slightly uphill between rocky outcrops. The car park comes into view very shortly after this turn. The path now descends diagonally towards the car park. Continue along until you reach a broad and steep grass slope. Turn left and descend to the road, turn right and return to the car park.*

Public Transport

It is difficult to reach the starting point of this walk by public transport. The alternatives are British Rail to Foxfield or Ribble Motor Services to Broughton-in-Furness. Thereafter there is only the Post Bus into the valley, and that leaves the Post Office in Broughton at 7.30 am.

The hogghole, allowing sheep to slip from field to field (route 3).

22

Grading: Moderate

Elter Water Round

Outline

Elterwater village – Great Langdale Beck – Elter Water – River Brathay – Skelwith Force – Skelwith Bridge – Colwith – Hacket – Slate Quarries – Elterwater village.

Summary

A longish walk which passes through a pleasant and gentle landscape of water, fields and woodland, but with good views of the surrounding fells. There are a few uphill stretches but they are very moderate. In general the going is good and the route easy to follow. The instructions seem complicated but route-finding is easier on the ground than it reads on the page.

Attractions

The first section follows Great Langdale Beck as it meanders through the valley into Elter Water. Shortly after Elter Water the River Brathay falls dramatically at Skelwith Force where it thrusts over a rocky ridge and swirls into a wide pool. The falls are set among ancient woodland of oak, birch, alder and beech with frequent plantations of coppiced hazel.

After the Force the route leads through the Kirkstone Quarry yard where slabs of the local green slate await use. There is an area to picnic at Skelwith Bridge where chaffinches will scavenge for crumbs of food.

A short section of road is followed by a stretch across more open countryside through Low and High Colwith and on to Low and High Hacket. A detour to Colwith Force is possible (though not included in the instructions). Towards the end of this section you are presented with one of the classic views of the Lake District where the majestic Langdale Pikes stand sentinel to Elter Water.

The last part of the route takes you through more old woodland before descending through slate quarries where massive piles of discarded slate stand behind high drystone walls. The final stretch takes you alongside Great Langdale Beck back into the village.

Refreshments

Cafes at Elterwater and Kirkstone Galleries.

Route 4

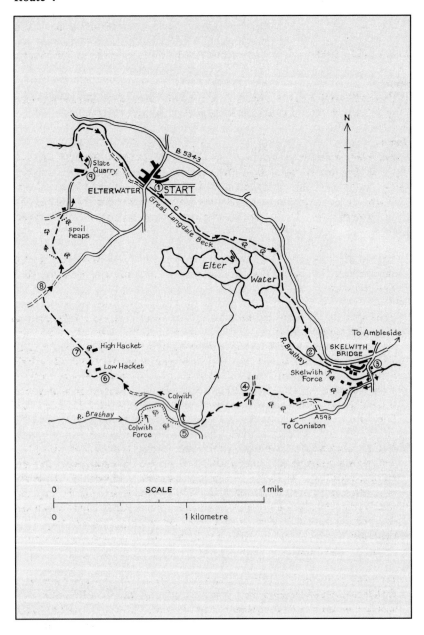

Route 4

Elter Water Round

Start

This walk starts from the car park alongside the Great Langdale Beck in the village of Elterwater. OS Outdoor Leisure, English Lakes SE (GR 328047).

Route

1. *Leave the car park by the kissing gate and follow the path to Skelwith Bridge. Cross two bridges and eventually leave the beckside to enter woodland. After a kissing gate the path continues across a field (which can be boggy) with the edge of Elter Water and the River Brathay on your right. When the river turns away to the right you carry on across the field, keeping to the left of a wooded knoll, towards a gate at the end of a drystone wall.*

2. *Shortly after passing through the gate and re-entering woodland take the right hand path at a fork and continue past Skelwith Force and through the slate works to Skelwith Bridge.*

3. *At Skelwith Bridge, turn right on to the A593, cross the bridge and follow the road round for 120 yards to the end of a row of cottages. Take the path on the right signposted to Colwith. Follow that through a kissing gate and a small woodland area to a farm track. Turn right towards the farm. Go through the gate close to the farm and follow the track to a stile with a waymark arrow. Cross the stile, go through a gap in the wall, and bear left to cross a beck and go through another gate. After 150 yards turn left onto another farm track signposted to Elterwater and Colwith.*

4. *Go through a gate into a farmyard, bear left across the front of a barn then right to pass between buildings as directed by a waymark arrow. Continue along the path, crossing a wall via a stile and a beck by stepping stones. Follow the path over two more stiles until a third is reached in front of a white painted house. Turn left and pass in front of the house to reach a metal kissing gate. Go through the gate and downhill to reach a stile. Cross the stile and descend steeply towards the river on your right. Carry on across a field to a slab stone stile set in a drystone wall. Cross the wall to join a road.*

5. *Turn right, signposted to Colwith Force and High Park (after 80 yards a path off to the left goes to Colwith Force). Stay on the road until a little way beyond a bridge then turn towards Little Langdale. Follow the road for 200 yards, then turn right*

Continued on page 26

*into a drive signposted as a public footpath. Go along the drive for 200 yards until another gate is reached. Go through the gate and turn left, cross a small beck and continue on with a stake and wire fence on your left. After 150 yards go through a gap in the drystone wall near to telegraph poles. Head towards a white-painted house (Low Hackett) visible two or three hundred yards ahead. (**Waymark arrows are frequent during the next section but are usually pointing back the way you have come.**)*

6. *Just before you reach the house there is a gap in a drystone wall on the left. Go through the gap. Keep the house on your right and carry on for 100 yards to some steps over a wall with a wooden rail on the top. (**This is not a barrier to deny you passage.**) Cross the wall and keep straight on to the next wall. Bear to the right and head for a gate in a wall ahead. Now head towards the wooden five-bar gate in a farm wall on a rise of ground ahead. About half way up the slope towards the farm turn left and aim for a gap in the wall about 100 yards away.*

7. *Go through the wall and carry on towards a rocky outcrop with another wall. Climb the steps over the wall and cross the field heading toward a gate in a stake and wire fence.*

8. *Go through the gate and turn right onto a track. After 150 yards go through another gate and turn immediately left off the track and slightly uphill on a path through woodland. (**If you wish you can return direct to Elterwater by carrying straight on along the track.**) After about 150 yards the path forks alongside a decaying wall. Keep to the right and descend until you reach a track close to a house. Turn right onto the track and then left immediately after the house onto a bridleway. Follow the bridleway down into the quarry and bear right as you enter the quarry yard.*

9. *Turn left at the end of the long sheds and descend on a roadway for 50 yards. Just as you pass under an overhead power cable bear to the left off the roadway and onto a path, keeping a house on your right. Follow the path down until you reach the river and turn right. Continue alongside the river until the path ascends to join a track. Turn left and descend into Elterwater.*

Public Transport
Ribble Motor Services from Ambleside.

Route 5 .... 3 miles

Grading: Easy

Glenridding and Lanty's Tarn

Outline
Glenridding Beck – Lanty's Tarn – Mires Beck – Glenridding Beck.

Summary
A short walk over rolling landscape which affords fine views across the head of Ullswater and up the Glenridding Screes. A small tarn is visited. The descent back into Glenridding is a good clear route which can be safely followed in poor light, making this an excellent walk for an evening's excursion.

Attractions
Set amidst the lower slopes of the fells behind Glenridding, Lanty's Tarn is a peaceful small haven. It is just off the path to Helvellyn by the Striding Edge route and is usually ignored by those seeking the challenge of the higher ground.

Glenridding was for many years a mining village. Lead was discovered nearby in the 1650s and by the late 1840s the mine at Greenside was the largest in the country. The information centre in the car park contains a small but informative exhibition on the industrial history of the valley.

The first part of the walk takes you slightly uphill alongside Glenridding Beck, and through wooded slopes. After habitation is left behind and more open country reached the attractions of this short walk become obvious. The head of Ullswater is surrounded by some of the most striking scenery in the lakes and the view before you changes as the direction of the walk alters.

Lanty's Tarn takes its name from the diminutive of Lancelot. Which Lancelot is long forgotten, but it was not he of the Lake. It sits, surrounded by trees, in a small hollow between crags, and is a pleasant spot to rest for a few minues after the climb. Thereafter the walk takes you over undulating landscape, dotted with crags and becks and with splendid views towards St. Sunday Crag and the rugged screes of Sheffield Pike.

Glenridding itself has many attractions. It can be reached by steamer from Pooley Bridge and Howtown. Rowing boats can be hired and it is possible to row out to the islands in the lake.

Refreshments
There are several pubs and cafes in Glenridding.

Route 5

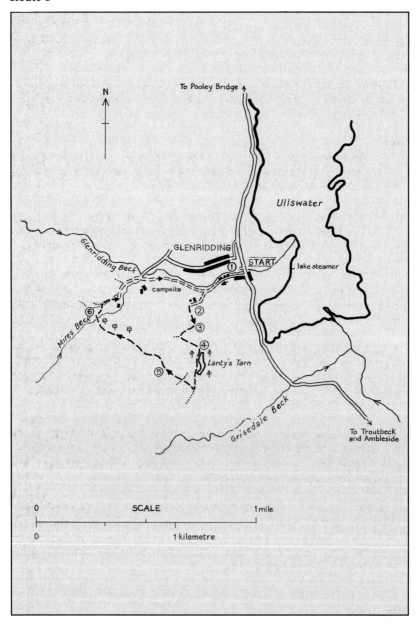

Route 5

Grading: Easy

Glenridding and Lanty's Tarn

3 miles

Start

From the car park in the centre of Glenridding. On Lake Ullswater 1 mile north-west of Patterdale on the A592. OS Outdoor Leisure, English Lakes NE (GR 385169).

Route

1. *From the car park entrance turn right, cross the bridge and turn immediately right onto a drive (signposted as a dead end) alongside Glenridding Beck. Follow the path for 300 yards until it forks. Take the left fork.*

2. *After a further hundred yards the path divides with each route waymarked, keep straight ahead passing cottages on your right. Bear left over a small footbridge with a gate at the far end and continue uphill through the trees to another gate.*

3. *Go through the gate, turn right and continue on until you reach another gate in a drystone wall. Turn left, signposted to Striding Edge & Grisedale, just before the gate. A further 300 yards brings you to yet another gate at the edge of Lanty's Tarn.*

4. *Keep the tarn on your left and follow the path alongside it. Just after the dam the path starts to descend. 150 yards downhill there is a grass path off to the right just opposite a 5-bar gate in a drystone wall – take this grass path uphill. After 200 yards take the right fork and aim towards a gate and stile in the drystone wall ahead and to your left.*

5. *Cross the stile and bear to the left as you pass round crags. The path follows the contour of the fellside and at first is not very distinct but it becomes clearer after a few hundred yards. Descend to meet another path alongside Mires Beck, keeping a drystone wall and woodland on your right.*

6. *Cross the beck and turn right, carry on until you reach a ladder stile on your right. Cross the stile and continue downhill on a broad path. Turn left beside a cottage and continue downhill. Just before Glenridding Beck turn right onto a path signposted to the car park. After 500 yards this joins the path passed at point 2 above. Turn left and retrace your steps back to the car park.*

Public Transport

Ribble Motor Services from Penrith or Ambleside.

Lanty's Tarn in winter.

Old lead mining wagons, Glenridding.

Grading: Moderate with one, avoidable, difficult stretch.

Gowbarrow Fell and Aira Force

Outline

Aira Force car park – Lyulph's Tower – Yew Crag – Shooting Lodge – Gowbarrow Fell – (Dockray) – High Force – Aira Force car park.

Summary

The walk described starts from the National Trust car park for Aira Force on the A592 alongside Ullswater. This can be very busy at peak times so an early start is recommended. There is another car park available a mile up the A5091 towards Dockray.

Throughout this area the walking is generally easy and full of interest. The first stretch of the route takes you across Aira Beck and through woodland to the foot of Yew Crag. This is ascended by way of slab steps which can be hazardous when wet and have been known to cause problems for people who suffer from vertigo. If this ascent might bother you take the higher path above Lyulph's Tower. Thereafter a long stretch of easy walking round the fellside with a short pull up to the summit of Gowbarrow Fell. There is then a short and steepish descent which joins up with the path that wends its way through the gorge and past Aira Force. To visit Dockray (and a pub with excellent ice-cream) requires a detour of half a mile each way.

Attractions

Gowbarrow Fell (1579 feet) stands on the shore of Ullswater, regarded by many as the most beautiful of the lakes. On the western side of the fell is the wonderful gorge of Aira Beck which contains the waterfall of Aira Force. This fall of 65 feet makes it the fourth highest in the district.

The ascent of Yew Crag makes use of a Victorian rock staircase which twists and turns up the cragside and it is not unusual to find yourself walking, carefully, close to crags where rock climbers practise their sport.

The open landscape leading from Yew Crag to the summit is a delightful area in which to wander with plenty of good picnic spots and the ruins of a shooting lodge to explore. The summit area itself is somewhat bleak and can live up to the meaning of its name "the windy hill".

The walk down alongside Aira Beck is quite simply enchanting.

Refreshments

Cafe at Aira Force car park or the Royal Hotel at Dockray.

Route 6

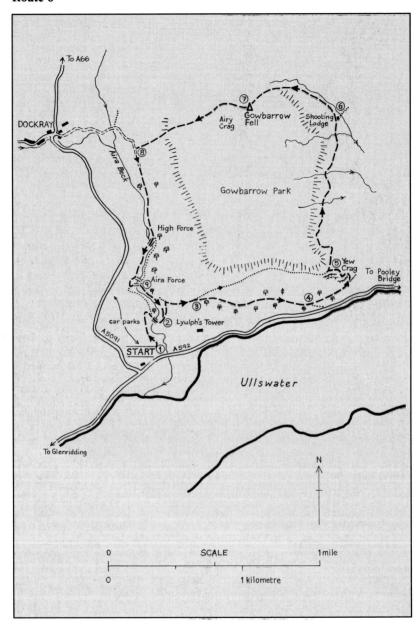

Route 6

Grading: Moderate with one difficult stretch

Gowbarrow Fell and Aira Force $6\frac{1}{2}$ miles

Start

From the National Trust car park (price £1, members free) 4 miles north of Patterdale on the A592 alongside Ullswater. OS Outdoor Leisure, English Lakes NE (GR 401201).

Route

1. *Leave the car park through the gate in the corner diagonally opposite the entrance and go along the track. Turn right through a gate, continue along the path and cross Aira Beck by the wooden footbridge. Climb the steps on the opposite bank.*

2. *Just after the top of the steps take a path off to the right and cross the stake and wire fence by a stile. Carry on for about 20 yards until the path forks. Take the right hand path and carry on for another 100 yards until the path forks again just above a castellated house called Lyulph's Tower.* **To avoid the climb up Yew Crag take the left hand, uphill, path.** *Then continue from 5 below.*

3. *Take the lower, right-hand, path and carry on through woodland for half a mile.*

4. *When the path next forks take the left-hand path uphill and continue on until, on your left, a series of rock steps are reached. Go up these to ascend Yew Crag. It is steep but somewhat eased by the zigzag route taken.* **Great care should be taken if the rocks are wet.** *At the top of the steps cross a stile and turn left and follow the stake and wire fence steeply uphill to another stile which gives access to the summit cairn.*

5. *From the summit, and with your back to the lake, turn right and follow the path around the fellside for half a mile, crossing three becks (the last by way of a wooden footbridge) until you arrive at the ruins of a shooting lodge.*

6. *The path now bears away left from the ruins, still keeping to the fellside and more or less parallel with a drystone wall on your right until the summit of Gowbarrow Fell becomes visible. Continue on and up to the summit.*

7. *From the summit cairn head towards the drystone wall and then bear left. Descend down Airy Crag keeping alongside the wall, past a small group of derelict buildings and on until a stone stile crosses another wall.*

Continued on page 34

33

8. *200 yards after the stile a signposted footpath is reached.* **Either** *Turn right to visit Dockray, returning thereafter to this point,* **Or** *Turn left and continue for half a mile through woodland until the wooden footbridge at High Force is reached. Cross the bridge, turn left and continue downstream until you reach the steps which lead down to Aira Force Lower Bridge.*

9. *From the lower bridge continue downstream until you meet the footbridge crossed soon after the start and return to the car park.*

Public Transport
Ribble Motor Services.

Hollow tree near Aira Beck

Hallin Fell

Outline
St. Peter's Church – Hallin Fell Summit – Geordie's Crag – Kailpot Crag –
Hallinhag Wood – Sandwick Bay – Hause Farm – St. Peter's Church.

Summary
This is a very good walk for children and includes a climb to the summit of the fell.
Hallin is 1271 feet high but requires only 700 feet of ascent due to the starting height.
Only the first few hundred yards are steep. The descent by the recommended route is
safe in all weather conditions although the grass of the lower slopes can be slippery.
The circuit round the fell is easy walking over gentle terrain with the exception of a
short, though steep, uphill section two-thirds of the way round.

Attractions
The summit of Hallin Fell overlooks Ullswater with excellent views of the lake and
surrounding mountains. The summit itself is a broad flat plateau dominated by the
summit cairn, a massive obelisk which is a monument to the dedication (or folly) of
whoever built it. After descending from the summit the route takes you around the
skirts of the fell beginning with a section around the northern side in open country.
The path along the western edge includes Geordie's Crag which is a good spot for
scrambling but take care as the side is steep and the lake is deep! Shortly afterwards
you reach Kailpot Crag and the small bay alongside which provides both
scrambling and a good place to picnic.

The walk continues through Hallinhag Wood towards Sandwick Bay where a
short detour from the route provides another good place to stop.

The final section after you leave the wood is across open scrubland before
passing Hause Farm to return to the starting point.

It is possible to start from Howtown which is reached by lake steamer from
either Glenridding or Pooley Bridge. It is essential to find out the steamer times and
allow plenty of time for it is a long walk back if you miss the last one.

If you go by car the old church of St. Martin in Martindale is worth a detour.

Refreshments
There are two pubs, both of which do food, and a cafe in Pooley Bridge and several
in Glenridding. Tea, coffee, soft drinks, snacks, etc. are also sold on the steamer.

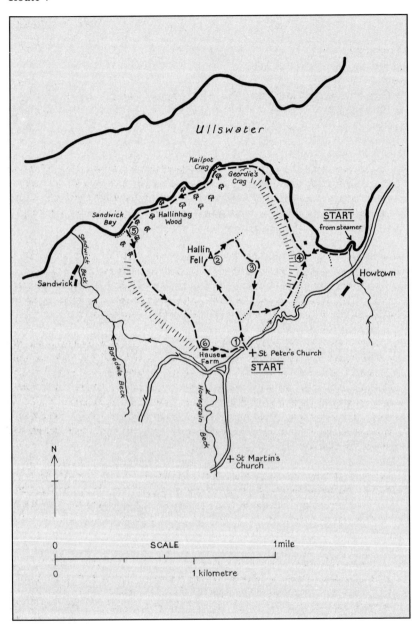

Route 7

Grading: Moderate

Hallin Fell   **4 miles**

Start

From St. Peter's Church (there is a parking area in front) on the eastern side of Ullswater between Howtown and Martindale 5 miles south of Pooley Bridge. OS Outdoor Leisure, English Lakes NE (GR 435191).

Route

1. *Opposite the front of St. Peter's Church take the broad grass path steeply uphill keeping a drystone wall on your left. Just after the wall ends the path forks. Keep to the left hand path and continue uphill until you come below and alongside two cairns on a ridge to your right. Keep straight on past these and the summit cairn soon comes into view. Bear right up towards it.*

2. *From the summit and looking towards the northern end of Ullswater, descend towards the north-east keeping two cairns, which are some way above the path, on your left. When you are alongside the first cairn the path forks, keep left and carry on downhill. About 150 yards after passing the second cairn turn right and continue on towards another cairn visible on a knoll some 300 yards ahead.*

3. *From the summit of this knoll (and assuming your back is to the summit of the fell) turn right and carry on for a few yards to the edge of a cairned ridge to join a broad grass path. Turn left on to the path and descend. The church soon comes into view and, as you descend towards it, turn left when the path forks. Follow this path until it meets another coming from the road on your right. Turn left onto this path from the road and carry on for 300 yards, keeping a drystone wall on your right, until a gateway in the wall is reached. (**The steps here lead down to the lakeside path and on to Howtown landing stage.**)*

4. *Carry on past the gate, keeping the drystone wall and a large house on your right. Follow the path around the fellside to Geordie's Crag. Continue on through a gate into Hallinhag Wood. Go through the wood keeping to the path near the lakeside, pass through an opening in a drystone wall and carry on until you come to another gate.*

5. *Just beyond this gate is Sandwick Bay, if you wish to detour there. If not, turn left before the gate and go steeply uphill keeping the drystone wall on your right. Go through a gate and follow the path until it forks. Keep to the right alongside the drystone wall until it turns away downhill. Here you keep straight on towards*

Continued on page 38

another wall 100 yards or so ahead. Bear right when you reach this wall and continue alongside it for 150 yards until you come to a stile on your left.

6. *Go over the stile and cross the field to a gate with a waymark arrow. Go through the gate and follow the contour of the slope towards a 5-bar gate in the far boundary wall. Cross this wall through a small wall-gate alongside the 5-bar gate and continue on towards the church.*

Howtown start variation

START from the landing stage GR 443199. Cross the footbridge and follow the path along the lake edge through 2 gates. After the second gate turn right and follow a gravel drive to a private gate. Turn left through a kissing gate and up the steps 100 yards ahead. Turn right through the gate at the top. This meets the route above at point 4. Then follow 5, 6, 1, 2, and 3 until you return to the top of the steps. Retrace your route to the landing stage.

Public Transport

Water: Ullswater Navigation & Transit Co.

Innominate Tarn.

Grading: Hard

Hay Stacks and Innominate Tarn

Outline
Gatesgarth Farm – Scarth Gap Pass – Hay Stacks – Innominate Tarn –
Blackbeck Tarn – Dubs Quarry – Warnscale Bottom – Gatesgarth Farm.

Summary
A varied and interesting walk over mixed terrain with an enchanting summit ideal
for picnics and exploration. Several fine upland tarns and lots of rocky outcrops
make the summit area an ideal location for a pleasant stop. The paths throughout
are clearly defined and frequently cairned and the descent recommended is broad,
easily defined and safe.

Attractions
Hay Stacks is a fell whose name may be derived from the hay-stack like appearance
of many of its scattered tors or from the Norse *stakkr* meaning high rocks. Standing
at approximately 1900 feet high it is dominated by larger neighbours. These
however cannot detract from the fell's own special magic. The route crosses the
valley bottom at the eastern end of Buttermere lake before ascending steeply for the
first 800 or so yards. Thereafter the climb is more gradual to Scarth Gap Pass. The
plateau plays host to a variety of upland flora including tormentil and heather. The
summit includes a charming small tarn which comes as a pleasant surprise as the
crest of the final rock band is reached. The whole area is a fine place for exploration
so long as the sharp descents to either side are kept firmly in mind. The section of the
walk from the summit to the old quarry at Dubs passes the delightfully named
Innominate Tarn. After the tarn the path skirts around Green Crag before crossing
open land towards Dubs Quarry. A detour to visit the quarry is well worthwhile if
you have a fascination for the quiet solemnity of places which once rang to the
sound of violent and demanding activity. As you descend and look up to the left at
the mountain you have just climbed you will be impressed. The sunless northern
crags make this enchanting fell seem more forbidding than it is.

Refreshments
Two pubs and a cafe in Buttermere village, $1\frac{1}{2}$ miles to the west, offer a selection of
food. There is frequently an ice-cream van at Gatesgarth where, it should be noted,
there are no toilets.

Route 8

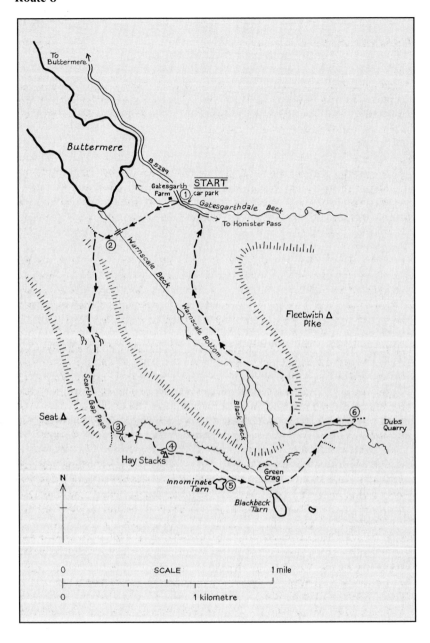

Route 8

Grading: Hard

Hay Stacks and Innominate Tarn   6 miles

Start

Car park (cost £2) at Gatesgarth Farm, alongside Gatesgarthdale Beck on the B5289 at the south eastern end of Buttermere lake, one and a half miles south east of Buttermere village and at the western end of the Honister pass. OS Outdoor Leisure, English Lakes NW (GR 195149).

Route

1. *Leave the car park, cross the road and take the footpath marked "Lakeside Path" on the gate alongside a post-box. Follow the path past the farm buildings and into open country, heading towards a drystone wall which descends almost vertically on the fellside ahead. Go through a gate and over a small wooden footbridge until a second gate is reached.*

2. *Once through this gate go uphill bearing to the right, signposted to Ennerdale via Scarth Gap. Follow the stake and wire fence uphill, turn left with the fence and continue uphill until a gate and stile are reached. Pause for a breather here, you are past the worst bit! Continue uphill towards the gap in the ridge ahead between two sets of crags and then along a distinct path occasionally marked with cairns.*

3. *At the top of Scarth Gap Pass the main mass of Haystacks is clearly visible to your left and is far less daunting than it appears. The path follows a cairned route across a grass and heather covered plateau. Bear round to the left as the ground begins to slope down towards the Ennerdale valley and take the zigzag path upwards and over a rocky band. After this band there is a small grass covered stretch before the final rock band which gives onto the summit. Keep to the left as you scramble up the final band.*

4. *Go ahead, off the rock band, around the charming summit tarn and onto the crag just ahead. The ridge of this small crag, about 50 yards long, has a cairn at each end. Authorities differ as to which is highest, I prefer the southerly one on the Ennerdale side, but touch both to be sure. The descent leaves the summit and follows a distinct path from the northern cairn and heads towards a tarn about a quarter of a mile ahead. This is the delightfully named and wonderfully situated Innominate Tarn.*

5. *From Innominate Tarn the path slopes downwards past occasional cairns before descending more steeply into a gully and past some impressive rock formations. Cross Black Beck and take the central path uphill and through some rocky outcrops. After the outcrops, keep to the right ignoring a more obvious looking*

Continued on page 42

route to the left – it leads to a dead end. The path then descends over grassy terrain towards a quarry spoil heap some distance ahead. The main path down can be seen descending to the left from the quarry workings.

6. *Just after crossing Warnscale Beck take the broad path downhill alongside the beck. This is an old quarry road and a safe and broad descent back into Warnscale Bottom. Stay on this path until the road is reached a few yards east of the car park.*

Public Transport available to Buttermere village only
Cumberland Motor Services from Cockermouth or Mountain Goat Bus Co. (April to end of September only) from Keswick.

Sheep in High Tilberthwaite.

42

Grading: Easy

High Tilberthwaite and Little Langdale

Outline
Hodge Close – Holme Ground – High Tilberthwaite – Moss Rigg Wood – River Brathay – cathedral cave – Little Langdale – Stang End – Little Fell – Hodge Close.

Summary
An excellent low level walk through mixed woodland in one of the loveliest areas of the district. For the most part the route follows clearly defined footpaths and tracks with only a short section on a road. A fine cave, part of a disused quarry complex, is visited.

Attractions
High Tilberthwaite and Little Langdale is an area where slate has been both mined and quarried from the 18th century. The archaeology of the industrial past of the region is still clearly visible in the landscape today where vast cavernous holes, huge spoil heaps and derelict buildings litter the area. Yet, time and a proliferation of vegetation have served to soften what would otherwise have been ugly scars.

    The walk starts from a flat area alongside Hodge Close quarry where the massive hole and its deep lake can be visited via a scramble down the old access ramp. After High Tilberthwaite the route wends through mixed wood and old quarry spoil heaps to the River Brathay. Here a short detour includes a visit to the magnificent cavern of the quarry mine at Little Langdale. The central cave, sometimes called the cathedral cave, is entered via a short tunnel which leads into the main area where a massive pillar of rock supports the roof. It is indeed not unlike the nave of a cathedral. This whole area is a mass of steep cliffs, deep holes, tunnels and caves and is worthy of close exploration. It is however potentially hazardous and great care must be taken all the time.

    From the river a short walk brings you into the hamlet of Little Langdale and the Three Shires Inn. The hamlet sits at the foot of the Wrynose Pass and the inn takes its name from the area at the top of the pass where, before Westminster decreed otherwise, the three counties of Cumberland, Westmorland and Lancashire met. Well-behaved children are welcome in the bar until 9.30 in the evening.

Refreshments
The Three Shires Inn at Little Langdale and a tea shop at Hodge Close.

Route 9

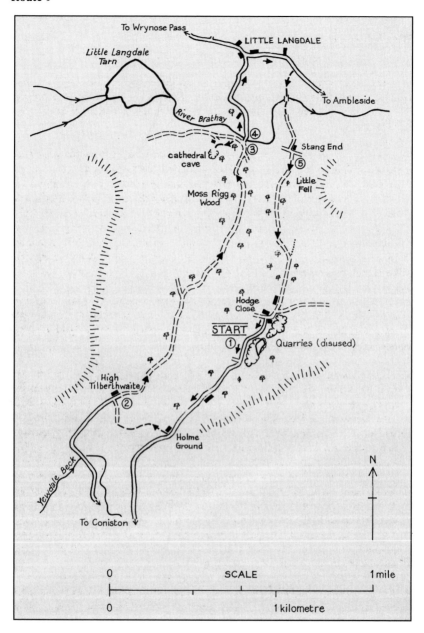

To Wrynose Pass

LITTLE LANGDALE

Little Langdale Tarn

To Ambleside

River Brathay

④

Stang End

③

cathedral
cave

⑤

Little
Fell

Moss Rigg
Wood

Hodge
Close

START

①

Quarries (disused)

High
Tilberthwaite

②

Holme
Ground

Yewdale Beck

To Coniston

N

0	SCALE	1 mile
0		1 kilometre

Route 9

Grading: Easy

High Tilberthwaite and Little Langdale   4 miles

Start

From the quarry at Hodge Close 1½ miles up the unnumbered road signposted to Hodge Close Only. This lies 3½ miles south of Skelwith Bridge on the A593 between Ambleside and Coniston. OS Outdoor Leisure, English Lakes SW (GR 315017).

Route

1. *From the level area used for parking go back along the road to the National Trust farm at Holme Ground. From the front of the farmhouse take the footpath signposted to High Tilberthwaite Only. Cross the field, bearing diagonally to the left to a narrow stile hole in the drystone wall. Once through (and it can be a tight squeeze) turn immediately left and go downhill to a gate in a stake and wire fence. Go through the gate and cross the field to a wooden gate at the end of a drystone wall. Follow the track alongside the drystone wall until the next gate is reached alongside a farm road. Go through that gate, turn right and carry on into and through the farmyard.*

2. *At the far end of the farmyard take the right hand track and follow it to a plateau on a spoil heap. 200 yards after the plateau, and when the path forks, take the right hand downhill track and follow that through Moss Rigg Wood until you reach the bridge over the River Brathay.*

3. *Turn left and, with the river on your right, follow the path for 75 yards until stretcher stones acting also as steps allow you to climb over the wall. Take the left hand path uphill to reach a plateau. Cross the plateau towards the stone hut and after 100 yards go through the tunnel on your left. The tunnel is about 20 yards long and there are stepping stones but, especially after heavy rain, a number can be just below the surface. However the water is rarely more than a few inches deep. This leads into the cathedral cave which, due to the large opening of a higher level is quite well lit. The water in the cave can be very deep so take care and keep to the edges. To leave the cave go through the small tunnel at the opposite end. You should now be at the bottom of the quarry bowl. Scramble up to the next level and have a wander round. To leave the quarry, either retrace your steps through the tunnel or scramble up the steep rock slope opposite the cave and turn right at the top to descend past two derelict buildings to the stone hut and thence back onto the plateau. Retrace your steps to the bridge.*

4. *Cross the bridge and follow the track until a road is reached. Turn right and follow the road for 250 yards until, on your right, a footpath alongside a small private*

Continued on page 46

parking enclosure at Greenbank is reached. Go through the kissing gate and cross the field to the narrow footbridge over the river. Cross that and head for a stile and gate ahead and slightly uphill to the left. Go over the stile and follow the track to the next gate beside the farm at Stang End. Go through the gate and turn left.

5. *Just past the end of the farmhouse take the track to the right and follow it until a signpost points a footpath to the left. You however turn right and go through a gate in a drystone wall to enter woodland. Follow the path through the wood to Hodge Close. Follow the path, which is now tarmacked, to the parking area.*

6. ***To visit the quarry at Hodge Close**, locate the slipway at the northern edge. Make your way down to the far end and go through the huge arch onto the jetty to view the quarry and lake. Do not be surprised to have scuba divers beneath your feet and rock climbers above your head.*

Public Transport
None.

The Bowder Stone.

46

Grading: Moderate

The Jaws of Borrowdale

Outline
Bowderstone car park – Bowder Stone – Frith Wood – Rosthwaite – River Derwent – New Bridge – High Hows Wood – Grange – Cummacatta Wood – car park.

Summary
A superb walk over easy terrain with only small climbs through varied landscape in what is perhaps the best known Cumbrian valley. The early part incorporates a visit to the Bowder Stone before continuing through woodland to the village of Rosthwaite. The route then passes through cultivated landscape before joining the River Derwent. More woodland then follows before a stretch over a rough track and quiet roadway brings you to Grange. The final section passes close to more woodland and bog.

Attractions
This walk takes you through the Jaws of Borrowdale where steep cliffs separate Derwent Water from the narrow cultivated area of Borrowdale. This was an area held in awe by 18th century writers and even today the wooded slopes and heather-covered upper reaches do little to lessen the stark angularity of the surrounding cliffs. The first port of call must be the Bowder Stone, a huge boulder which in the 19th century was claimed to be the largest in the world. Steps provide easy access to the top.

Parts of the walk take you through ancient woodlands at Frith and High and Low Hows woods where oak, birch, hazel, alder and ash bear witness to both ancient and modern forestry and provide a habitat for a wide variety of flora and fauna. Herons, pied flycatchers and woodpeckers may be seen. Plants such as the insectivorous sundew, grass of parnassas and wood sorrell may be spotted and fungi such as the poisonous fly agaric.

The disused quarry in High Hows Wood is worth a closer inspection if only to see the pigmentation of the rocks. Shortly afterwards a wide bend in the river makes a pleasant place to picnic.

The final part of the walk, through an open area in Cummacatta Wood, also passes a quarry with a cave.

Refreshments
In Rosthwaite (nearly halfway round) there is a general store which sells ice cream and soft drinks and a hotel which serves morning coffee and bar food. There are also two cafes in Grange.

Route 10

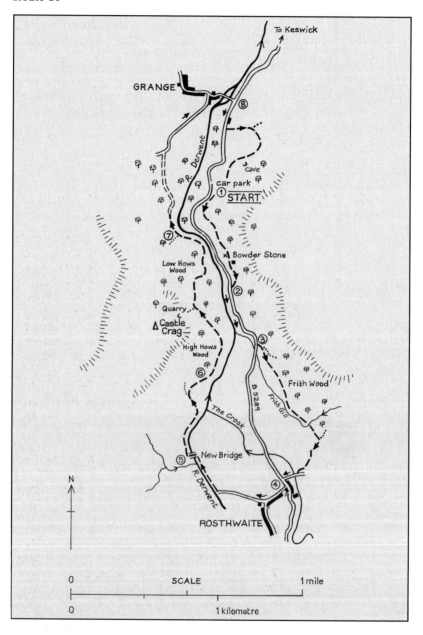

Route 10

The Jaws of Borrowdale
$4\frac{1}{2}$ miles

Start

From the National Trust Bowder Stone car park on the B5289 4 miles south of Keswick (members free). OS Outdoor Leisure, English Lakes NW (GR 253168).

Route

1. *Leave the car park near the main entrance and turn left onto the footpath signposted to the Bowder Stone. From the Stone follow the path between two buildings. Descend to join the road. Cross to the footpath on the opposite side.*

2. *Continue on the footpath for several hundred yards until you reach a small drystone walled square clearing on the opposite side of the road.*

3. *Cross to the clearing, go through the gate and turn right. (There is a National Trust namepost for Grange Fell a few yards down the path.) Follow the path along the edge of Frith Wood until you reach a gate. Go through the gate and shortly afterwards the path runs alongside Frith Gill. Continue alongside the gill for 250 yards until the gill bends sharply to your left. Cross the gill, go through the gate a few yards ahead and follow an indistinct path for 200 yards, keeping a stake and wire fence on your right, until you meet a broad footpath. Turn right onto this path, go downhill for 50 yards and turn left through a gate, then follow the track until a roadway is reached. Turn right, go over a hump-back bridge and on to the main road. Turn left into Rosthwaite.*

4. *Turn right off the main road towards Yew Tree Farm. Go through the farm and follow the path signposted to Grange. Turn right when you meet the river and cross it at New Bridge.*

5. *At the far end of the bridge turn right, go on for 100 yards and cross over a stile on the right-hand side of two 5-bar gates (just to confuse things, both are marked footpath!). With the river on your right follow the path until it turns left away from the river near a stand of trees on a rocky knoll. Continue on until you reach a gate at the edge of a wood.*

6. *Go through the gate and carry on for 300 yards until the path forks. Take the left-hand path to and through an old quarry. At the far end of the quarry, turn right when you meet another path. Carry on downhill until you reach a hole in a drystone wall. Turn right after the wall and follow the path, cross a stake and wire fence by a stile and 100 yards further on arrive at a junction of paths alongside a wide bend in the river.*

Continued on page 50

7. *Follow the path alongside the river for a few yards. It then climbs uphill slightly and becomes a rough track with a drystone wall on your right. Follow this until you reach a metalled road. Turn right and stay on this road until you reach Grange. Turn right, go through Grange, cross the bridge and carry on to the B5289.*

8. *Turn right towards Rosthwaite & Seatoller. After 150 yards there is a stile in the stake and wire fence on the opposite side of the road (a few yards after a house called Grange View). Cross this stile and climb uphill for 100 yards. At a fork take the left hand path, carry on for another 150 yards, passing under an overhead cable, and turn right onto a path which skirts the edge of a bog area. Continue on for 300 yards past the front of a quarry. The edge of the car park can then be seen some 200 yards ahead through the trees.*

Public Transport
Cumberland Motor Services from Keswick.

Keswick railway crossing the River Brathay via an inverted bow-string bridge (route 11).

Grading: Easy

Keswick Railway and Brundholme Woods

Outline
Keswick Station – Brigham – Low Biery – Brundholme Wood – River Greta – Keswick Station.

Summary
A very good walk for smaller children which, on the outward part, follows the line of a disused railway and crosses the River Greta several times by way of the rail bridges. The walking is level and easy and, at the appropriate season, can provide a good crop of wild strawberries. Once the railway is left behind the return leg goes on a permissive footpath through Brundholme Woods. A stretch alongside the River Greta is over rougher and more hilly terrain. This part of the route has occasional steep drops down to the river so an eye should be kept on children and a lead on dogs. Finally a short section of road and a few yards on a driveway lead to a short wooded section before the end.

Attractions
The disused railway line was part of the Cockermouth, Keswick and Penrith Railway which, prior to its closure in 1972, was regarded as one of the major scenic routes in the country. The area around the line has an interesting industrial history and several notice boards along the way provide information. The route passes Brigham and Low Briery where, from the 14th century, water has provided the power for a number of mills. A series of slender bow-string girder bridges then carry you high above the River Greta.

The section of the walk through Brundholme woods is delightful with a large variety of trees and wild flowers. The most common tree in the wood is the sessile oak with its stalkless acorns but many birch trees have colonized the more open areas. The wood is also one of the areas where you may catch sight of the native Red Squirrel. There are several suitable picnic spots alongside the river and it is possible to see dippers.

At the end of the walk you can enjoy a swim in the Keswick Spa pool complete with waterslide and wave machine. Refreshments are also served to swimmers.

Refreshments
Keswick has a wide range of cafes, restaurants and pubs.

Route 11

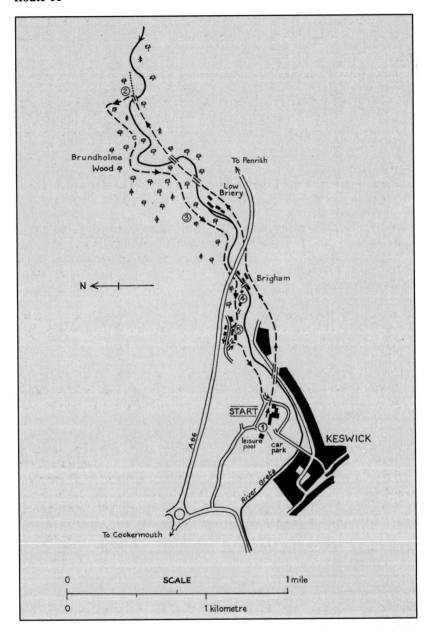

Route 11

Keswick Railway and Brundholme Woods

5 miles

Start

From the car park at the Keswick Spa leisure pool. Parking costs £1 but is free (on application for a token) to users of the pool. To reach the start from the town centre; go along Station Road, turn right into Brundholme Road and follow the road round until the swimming pool is reached. The station is 100 yards east of the pool and there is ample parking. OS Outdoor Leisure, English Lakes NW (GR 270238).

Route

1. *From the station go east following the line of the railway for 2½ miles. On the way you will cross and recross the River Gretta by way of 4 railway bridges.*

2. *At the eastern end of the fourth bridge turn left and cross a stile signposted to Keswick via Brundholme Wood. Keep a stake and wire fence on your left and go steeply uphill using a zigzag series of wooden steps until you reach a stile on your left. Cross the stile and take the path through the wood. The path is occasionally marked with posts.*

3. *At a junction of paths take the route signposted to Keswick. Continue on until you pass underneath the viaduct which carries the A66. A little further on and just before you reach a bridge turn right and go up wooden steps.*

4. *Turn left at the top of the steps and follow the path until you reach a wooden enclosure and riding stables. Bear to the right after the enclosure and carry on for a few yards until you reach a gravelled drive. Turn right and carry on for a few more yards until you reach a road.*

5. *At the road, alongside the Calvert Trust Adventure Centre, turn left and go downhill until a signpost directs you left to Keswick. Take this path, which for the first few yards is along the drive of the Brundholme Country Hotel. Turn right off the drive at the signpost to Keswick. Follow this path over 2 bridges and past a timeshare development. Go straight down the drive (it is an approved footpath) until a road is reached. Turn left at the road and take the steps, a few yards ahead and to your left, up the side of a railway bridge. Once atop the bridge turn right and retrace your steps back to the starting point.*

Public Transport

Keswick is well-served by public transport but mainly Cumberland Motor Services and National Travel.

Rock pillar supporting the roof of 'cathedral cave', Little Langdale (route 9).

Grading: Moderate with some hard ascent

Loughrigg Fell and Terrace

Outline

White Moss Common – Loughrigg Terrace – Loughrigg Summit – Big (or Rydal) Cave – White Moss Common.

Summary

A delightful walk on one of the finest of the minor gems of the Lake District fells. The route first passes through the wetlands of White Moss Common before following the terrace walk overlooking Grasmere lake. Then follows a steep but not unpleasant ascent to the summit area. The descent is also steep but, with care, can be safely followed through old quarry workings. A visit to a large cave is a good end to the descent which is followed by a gentle walk across the base of the northern face of the fell overlooking Rydal Water.

Attractions

Loughrigg seems a very modest fell being only 1101 feet high, but since it stands in splendid isolation it is in many ways the equal of its higher and more imposing neighbours. The first part of the walk takes you through the gentle landscape of the wetlands and woodlands of White Moss Common before opening out into the pleasant terrace walk with fine views over Grasmere lake and towards the mountains beyond. The climb to the summit calls for 925 feet of ascent in the $1\frac{1}{2}$ miles from White Moss Common. However, by the time you turn from the terrace the climb will have reduced to a little over 600 feet. The route to the summit follows the line of a ridge and takes you over several rocky outcrops. It is not too arduous, given a few stops for a breather, and provides wonderful views all the while. The summit itself is a splendid natural playground with rocky outcrops, grass knolls and a small tarn. You may well see jackdaws and meadow pipits and one of the finest panoramas the district has to offer.

The descent includes some derelict quarries and a small bog where you may find butterwort and the insectivorous sundew. It ends close to the splendid Big Cave, sometimes called Rydal Cave. This handsome feature encloses a small pond, sometimes visited by ducks, where paddling is possible at the edges. The final stretch covers the open ground overlooking Rydal Water.

Refreshments

Both Ambleside and Grasmere are well supplied with cafes and pubs.

Route 12

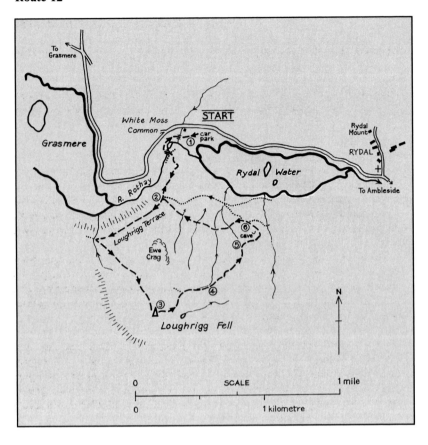

Route 12

Grading: Moderate with some hard ascent

Loughrigg Fell and Terrace

4 miles

Start

The walk starts from the car park at White Moss Common on the left side of the A591, 3 miles from Ambleside on the Keswick road. OS Outdoor Leisure, English Lakes SE (GR 351065).

Route

1. *Leave the car park by the gate alongside the map-board. Follow the path to a footbridge, cross this and continue alongside the River Rothay until you can cross it by a large footbridge. Take the central of 3 paths signposted as 'Woodland Walk to Viewpoints of Loughrigg Terrace'. Follow this path through the woods, taking the higher right-hand path when it forks, and continue on to a gate in a drystone wall.*

2. *Go through the gate, turn right and follow the terrace path round the edge of the fell. After about half a mile, just before you reach a drystone wall turn sharply left onto the uphill path. Keep on this path through the occasional rocky outcrops until you reach a distinct ridge. From the ridge follow the cairned path to the summit which is clearly visible ahead.*

3. *To descend from the summit start off to the left (i.e. east) of the summit cairn on a path which leads towards a grassy knoll about 100 yards away. Keep to the right to pass round the base. Continue on, passing a small tarn on your right, until the path forks. Take the centre path which ascends for a few yards towards a small ridge on the skyline. From this ridge the line of the descent is clearly visible before you as it works its way through disused quarries.*

4. *At the base of the first stretch of the descent make your way around a small boggy area and head towards a spoil heap ahead and to your right. At the edge of the spoil heap and alongside a cairn, turn right and, climbing gently continue on to the next spoil heap. As you get closer you will see a cairn and a derelict building. Follow the path round this on the left and carry on until you reach a beck which descends steeply downhill.*

5. *Cross the beck and carry on ahead until the path forks at an outcrop of rock. Take the left-hand path towards another larger outcrop (aim towards a white building on the opposite side of Rydal Water). Follow this path for 200 yards, bear right at the fork and after another 100 yards bear left. Follow this path for a few yards round and to the front of Big Cave.*

Continued on page 58

57

6. *From Big Cave head north-west and follow the terrace path as it contours the fellside back towards the drystone wall surrounding the wood you passed through shortly after the start. When the path forks near a semi-derelict barn, take the right-hand path towards the drystone wall aiming for the gate. Alternatively take the lower path alongside a drystone wall until you reach the gate. From the gate retrace your steps to the car park.*

Public Transport
National Travel or Ribble Motor Services from Ambleside or Grasmere.

Looking out from the big cave.

Grading: Hard

Skiddaw via Ullock Pike

Outline
Parking area – Kiln Pots – The Edge – Ullock Pike – Longside Edge –
Skiddaw – Broad End – Barkbeth Gill – Barkbethdale – Little Knott –
Parking area.

Summary
A demanding walk on ridge and open fellside climbing on a clearly defined path to
the summit of one of only four points in England with a height of over 3000 feet. The
descent is good though lengthy. The route is unquestionably arduous but much less
so than it appears either on the map or from the valley. The route we have selected is
a minor classic of mountain walks and should be within the compass of teenagers or
even slightly younger children of an adventurous nature.

Attractions
It seemed slightly improper to compile this anthology of walks in the Lake District
without including one of the four highest mountains. The two highest, Scafell Pike
and Scafell, are too demanding for the scope of this book, as is Helvellyn by the
finest route. Skiddaw dominates the northern area of the national park and is
formed from the oldest rock in the district, the Skiddaw group of Ordovician rocks.
The summit plateau is a rough stony ridge from which the magnificent panorama of
the Pennines, the Lake District, the Solway Firth and Scotland can be seen. The
summit of Ullock Pike, climbed on the way, provides a splendid view down
Borrowdale.

The route selected crosses farmland before following the ridge over the summit
of Ullock Pike (2230 feet) and along Longside Edge. Then on to a splendid diagonal
rake up the west face of Skiddaw to gain the summit plateau.

The descent follows the slope down and into Barkbethdale. The path then goes
around the head of the dale before continuing down it high above the gill. It is rather
a long way back and steep in parts though safe, and by following the cairns can be
negotiated in mist or bad weather.

Refreshments
Old Sawmill Cafe at Dodd's Wood (open April–October).

Route 13

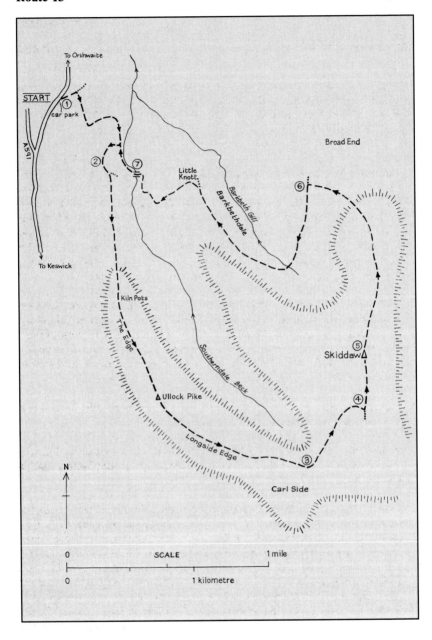

Route 13

Skiddaw via Ullock Pike   **8 miles**

Start

From a small area where a handful of cars can be parked on the right 500 yards along the narrow road to Orthwaite. The junction of this road with the A591 is 4.8 miles north of the roundabout on the A66 just outside Keswick. OS Pathfinder 576 Caldbeck and Outdoor Leisure, English Lakes NE (GR 236310).

Route

1. *Go through the gate by the bridlepath signpost, just beyond the parking area. Turn immediately left and cross the beck. After 200 yards turn right by a waymark arrow, and keeping the line of trees on your left, carry on to the next waymark arrow. Turn left as directed and cross over two drystone walls via ladder stiles. After the second the path bears to the right. Follow a grass track to a stile and gate at the edge of a drystone wall. Turn right after the stile and, keeping the wall on your right, carry on for 150 yards until a grass path goes off on your left. This path is roughly halfway between two ladder stiles over the wall on the right.*

2. *Follow this path around the right-hand side of a ridge for 200 yards until you meet a path which goes off to the right and up a small hillock to a cairn at the summit. Follow this path past the cairn and keep on until it joins the main ridge path and soon thereafter turns to a scree path. Follow the ridge path over the summit of Ullock Pike (2230 feet). From the summit continue along the ridge descending towards a col.*

3. *Turn left at the col and ascend the western flank of Skiddaw by following the broad scree rake to the summit plateau of Skiddaw (3053 feet).*

4. *At the summit plateau turn left to reach the northern, higher, summit marked by an OS triangulation point (though a detour of a couple of hundred yards to visit the south summit should not be missed).*

5. *To descend: from the triangulation point at the summit head north to the edge of the plateau about 200 yards ahead (keeping away from the steep eastern side). From the plateau edge descend heading in the general direction of a stake and wire fence ahead and to your right. After the first steep descent, locate the two cairns about 50 yards to the left of the fence. Follow the line of cairns down the flank of the fell. As a distant aid to direction you will soon be able to see a tarn a couple of miles ahead. Aim towards that until the cairns take you more to the left, when you should be heading towards a large plantation in the valley ahead. Continue down following*

Continued on page 62

the cairns until you meet a narrow path near the edge of the large heather covered area. (This is a little over a mile from the summit.)

6. *Turn left onto the path through the heather and follow it diagonally down into Barkbethdale. The path follows the line of the valley high above Barkbeth Gill. Stay on the path heading towards the drystone wall at the end of the valley. 200 yards from the wall a path off to the left will take you over Little Knott, follow it over and round to the right until you reach a small bridge over a beck and alongside a sheepfold. (If you miss this path, and it is a bit indistinct, don't worry, keep straight on to the wall and turn left when you reach it. Follow the wall down and just after it breaks away to your right you will see the bridge a little way ahead.)*

7. *Turn right after the bridge and carry on to the stile and gate at the end of the drystone wall which you passed during the ascent. Retrace your steps to the parking area.*

Public Transport
Cumberland Motor Services from Keswick to the end of the Orthwaite road.

Derwentwater and Borrowdale from Ullock Pike.

62

Grading: Hard

Stickle Tarn, Pavey Ark and Harrison Stickle

Outline

Car park – Stickle Ghyll – Stickle Tarn – Bright Beck – North Rake – Pavey Ark – Harrison Stickle – Dungeon Ghyll – Pike How – Car park.

Summary

A demanding walk with some steep ascents but throughout on good paths which provide one of the great ascents of the area. Suitable for older children or those a little younger with a sense of adventure.

The first section climbs alongside Stickle Ghyll to Stickle Tarn. Thereafter the route passes round the tarn and up a rocky gully on the edge of Pavey Ark. The summit of the fell is visited before the ridge is followed onto the summit of Harrison Stickle. From there a steep descent takes you into a hanging valley which in turn descends alongside the higher reaches of Dungeon Ghyll. Thereafter the route descends over open land towards Pike How before returning to the car park.

Attractions

The Langdale valley is one of the most beautiful areas in the Lake District. The walk itself provides a fine insight into features which are essential to an appreciation of Cumbrian landscape.

The early part of the walk takes you alongside Stickle Ghyll on an excellent and well marked path with a small section of rock-scrambling. The sudden appearance of Stickle Tarn at the end of this section is a pleasant surprise. The tarn is a popular excursion place and when seen dramatically displayed against the back-drop of Pavey Ark and Harrison Stickle, it is easy to understand why. From the tarn the mass of Pavey Ark looks awesome, though the ascent is easier than it first appears. The route taken is by way of a rocky gully on the edge of the mountain's mass. The views from the summits of Pavey Ark (2288 feet) and Harrison Stickle (2403 feet) are wonderful and the whole of the landscape from the tarn to the final descent is dramatic. Massive crags and precipices contrast with gaunt stretches of high moorland. It is a place of sombre beauty.

Refreshments

The Sticklebarn, alongside the car park, does a range of bar meals. In wet weather the roaring log fire can be very welcome.

Public Transport

Ribble Motor Services.

Route 14

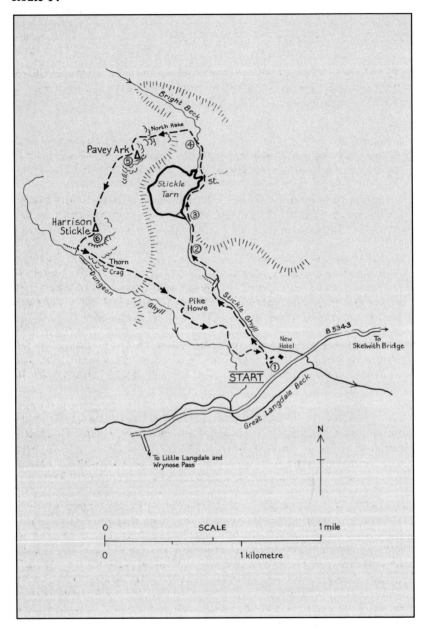

Route 14

Grading: Hard

Stickle Tarn, Pavey Ark and Harrison Stickle   5 miles

Start

> *This route is described from the National Trust car park close to the Dungeon Ghyll Hotel on the northern side of the B5343 towards the head of Great Langdale. OS Outdoor Leisure, English Lakes SW (GR 294064).*

Route

1. *From the car park leave by the steps alongside the noticeboard. Follow the path through a pair of gates. Bear right at a fork in the path and continue alongside the ghyll. Cross the footbridge and continue uphill on the right-hand bank.*

2. *Stay on the path until it runs out up against a rock slab. Scramble up the rocks following a natural fault which bears slightly to the right. After a scramble of about 30 feet turn left and continue to the tarn.*

3. *At the tarn turn right and continue round keeping it on your left. Cross over a boggy area, and a beck by stepping stones. 50 yards further on cross another small beck and, bearing to the left, carry on for a further hundred yards until you reach Bright Beck. Follow the path alongside the beck, keeping it on your left, for a further 250 yards until you reach a junction in the path marked by a small cairn.*

4. *Cross Bright Beck and continue up the scree path diagonally ahead and at the edge of the Pavey Ark buttress. This leads into the North Rake. Scramble up that and follow the cairned path towards the summit. Cross the drystone wall to reach the summit.*

5. *Leave the summit by retracing your steps over the drystone wall, then turn left towards Harrison Stickle. Keep to the ridge towards the Stickle. The path is marked by occasional cairns but can be difficult to discern as part of the route crosses bouldery ground. Keep as high as you comfortably can with the break of slope on your left and make your way onto the summit of Harrison Stickle.*

6. *Descend from the summit of Harrison Stickle by heading towards the south cairn about 60 yards from the top. The path down is clearly visible from the cairn. After passing over a rocky band the path descends towards a boggy area. When the path forks, turn left, aiming towards a ravine and follow the cairned path with Dungeon Ghyll on your right. Follow the narrow but clearly defined path alongside the ghyll and then down towards Pike How. Erosion control routes are in operation but the path is clearly posted. Follow the directed route downhill into the valley, passing over a drystone wall and on to a kissing gate. Rejoin the path followed at the start and retrace your steps into the car park.*

Pavey Ark from Stickle Tarn.

Route 15 $3\frac{1}{2}$ **miles**

Grading: Moderate

Stanley Ghyll and the River Esk

Outline
Dalegarth Station – St. Catherine's church – River Esk – new bridge – Stanley Ghyll – Stanley Force – stepping stones – St. Catherine's church – Dalegarth Station.

Summary
A short walk which visits St. Catherine's church, continues alongside the River Esk, ascends to the waterfall of Stanley Force and brings you back to Dalegarth by way of stepping stones across the river.

Attractions
One of the main attractions of this walk must be one method of reaching the starting point. Take the Ravenglass and Eskdale Miniature Railway from Ravenglass or Eskdale Green to the Terminus at Dalegarth. The "Ratty" has a 15-inch gauge track which was laid down in the 1870s to carry ore from the mines in Boot to Ravenglass. The line when faced with extinction in 1961 was taken over by a preservation society which continues to run the railway as a holiday attraction.

From the terminus at Dalegarth it is a gentle walk to the church of St. Catherine which stands alongside the River Esk and presents a fine example of a typical dale church with its low single chancel and nave.

Along the river there are many places to stop and picnic. After crossing by the new bridge you pass through mixed woodland and open areas to the wooded glade at the foot of Stanley Ghyll. The steep sided ravine is softened by the wide variety of ferns which festoon its walls. In late spring and early summer, when the rhododendron bushes are in flower, it is an enchanting place and in autumn when the leaves of the birch and larch turn colour it is vibrantly golden.

A clear view of the fall itself requires a hundred yards of scrambling at the apex of the walk and is best not attempted if the weather has made the ground slippery underfoot. The river is recrossed by some stepping stones close to the church but they also can be slippery when wet.

Refreshments
The cafe at Dalegarth station serves the usual array of soft drinks and snacks. Opening hours are a little erratic and related to the train timetable. A souvenir shop and toilets are also available on the station. Brook House, a licensed restaurant offering a wide range of good food, at the end of the lane from the church is also to be recommended.

Route 15

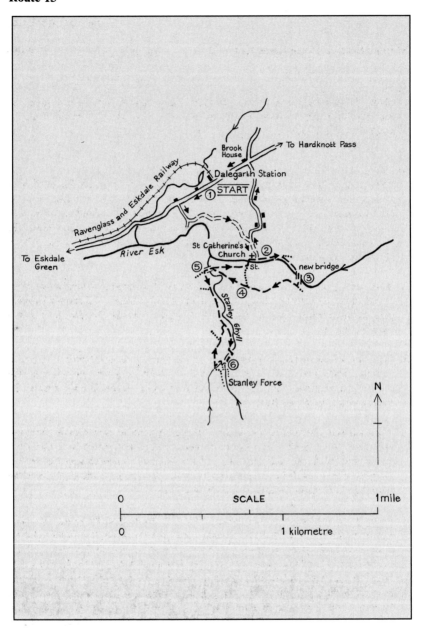

Route 15

Stanley Ghyll and the River Esk

$3\frac{1}{2}$ miles

Start

From the car park at Dalegarth Station, the terminus of the Ravenglass and Eskdale Miniature Railway, about 7 miles northeast of Ravenglass. OS Outdoor Leisure, English Lakes SW (GR 173006).

Route

1. *Turn right out of the car park and follow the road for 300 yards. Turn left onto another minor road opposite the Eskdale Centre (a War Memorial stands on the corner). Carry on up the roadway for 150 yards until, at a bend in the road, a bridleway leads off to the left at the end of a drystone wall. Continue along the bridleway until the junction with another track near to St. Catherine's church. Turn right towards the church.*

2. *At the end of the churchyard wall turn left and follow the path alongside the River Esk signposted to Doctors Bridge. Keep alongside the river until, just after a kissing gate, the path forks. Take the right-hand path closest to the river for 200 yards to the new bridge.*

3. *Cross the bridge, and just beyond the end, bear right up the bank towards a gate in a drystone wall. Turn right, go over the stile, and follow the path until you reach the corner of a drystone-walled enclosure on your right alongside a signpost to St. Catherine's church and Boot.*

4. *A few yards to the right of the signpost there is a gap in the wall, turn left here and head away from the enclosure. Cross an open area, fording a small beck, towards a drystone wall interspersed with stake and wire fencing 200 yards ahead. Go through the gate into a wooded area and continue on to a wooden footbridge. Cross the footbridge and make for a gate in a drystone wall.*

5. *Turn left before the gate and, keeping the wall on your right, go through the open woodland until a broad path is reached which ascends alongside Stanley Ghyll. Follow the path uphill alongside the ghyll which is crossed and recrossed by two footbridges until a third footbridge is reached. A small barrier at the far end of this bridge warns that the path ahead is unsafe. However, given sensible care it is possible to carry on from the end of the bridge for 100 yards to obtain a fine view of Stanley Force. **Under no circumstances is it either safe or wise to proceed further.***

Continued on page 70

69

6. *To descend: Return to the steps between the second and third bridges, climb these. Shortly after the top of the steps the path continues uphill. Follow it and take the right-hand path at a fork a little further on and descend to rejoin the main path used in the ascent. Retrace your route over the lower bridge and back to the gate in the drystone wall. Bear slightly to the left after the gate and continue to another gate, in a stake and wire fence, alongside the river.*

7. *Go through the gate and cross the river by the stepping stones (take care they can be slippery when wet) and on to the track which passes the church. Follow the track between drystone walls for $\frac{1}{2}$ mile until the road is reached. Turn left onto the road and return to the car park.*

Public Transport
British Rail or Cumberland Motor Services to Ravenglass then Ravenglass and Eskdale Miniature Railway to Dalegarth.

Stepping stones across the River Esk.

Grading: Easy

Wasdale Head

Outline
Car park – Lingmell Gill – Lingmell Fell foot – St. Olaf's Church –
Burnthwaite – Fogmire Beck – Mosedale Beck – Wasdale Head – Lingmell
Gill – Car park.

Summary
A walk which affords views of some of the highest mountains of the Lake District
whilst demanding only a moderate ascent which comes soon after the start. In the
first stages you walk towards the Scafell massif which terminates in the highest
mountain in England. A later section takes you towards Great Gable which many
walkers regard as the finest mountain. For a large part of the walk the village of
Wasdale Head is in view.

Attractions
The valley of Wasdale is particularly striking as it contains the sombre beauty of
Wastwater and the stark magnificence of the screes which fall from a great height
into the lake on the eastern side. The northern end of the valley is dominated by
Great Gable which, though not the highest mountain in England is perhaps the
most dramatic.

The small village of Wasdale Head is almost synonymous with the genesis of
English rock climbing for it was in the inn there where so many of "the first tigers"
stayed. In inclement weather they would amuse themselves by climbing around the
interior. In the 19th century one of the landlords was Will Ritson, notorious for his
fine disregard for the strict truth. It was claimed that Wasdale had the highest
mountain, deepest lake, smallest church and, in Ritson, the biggest liar in the land.
With his reputation for carelessness with the truth well-established, he once won a
lie-telling contest by claiming that he must withdraw from the competition because
"he could not tell a lie".

The church of St. Olaf is delightful in its size and simplicity. One of the smallest
in the county, it is a single nave and chancel structure which stands in a peaceful
graveyard amidst the graves of several climbers who have lost their lives on the
demanding faces of surrounding mountains.

Refreshments
The Wasdale Head Inn offers drinks, bar food and coffee (no tea or ice cream), and
toilets. A cottage, two doors from the hotel, serves teas.

Route 16

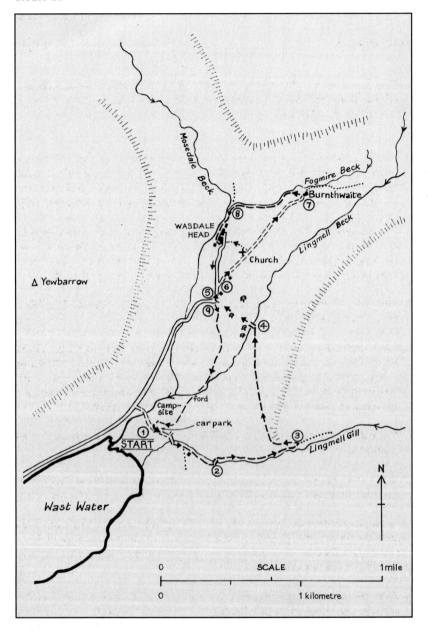

Route 16

Wasdale Head

$4\frac{1}{2}$ miles

Start

The route is described from the National Trust car park situated between the head of Wastwater and the village of Wasdale Head. OS Outdoor Leisure, English Lakes SW (GR 182074).

Route

1. *Turn left out of the car park and follow the track up to and across a wooden footbridge which crosses Lingmell Gill. Immediately after crossing the bridge take the left-hand footpath signposted to Eskdale and Scafell Route. At the next fork take the left-hand Permissive Footpath to Scafell, to a small wooden footbridge.*

2. *Cross Lingmell Gill by this bridge, go through the gate and follow the path uphill and through the next gate alongside the Scafell Massif cairn. Several hundred yards further on the path reaches a stile in a stake and wire fence a few yards in front of a drystone wall. Just before the stile there is another path on the left.*

3. *Take this path to the left (virtually a hairpin turn) and follow it around the fellside for a further $\frac{1}{2}$ mile to a gate in a drystone wall.*

4. *Go through the gate and cross Lingmell Beck via a wooden footbridge. Take a straight line from the end of the bridge across the field, keeping a large pile of stone on the left, and aim for the right hand edge of three large trees alongside a semi-derelict drystone wall. The path becomes more distinct again through a patch of gorse and continues on for 100 yards to a stile leading to the road.*

5. *Cross the stile and turn right towards Wasdale Head, walking alongside the road until the green is reached.*

6. *At the green keep to the right, along a Public Bridleway to Styhead Pass. Follow the track between drystone walls, past the church and on to Burnthwaite Farm.*

7. *At the farm keep to the left of the barn, go through the gate and turn immediately left following the path between drystone walls and repeatedly crossing the beck by a series of small wooden footbridges. After 300 yards this path is joined by another coming from the right.*

8. *Turn right at this junction of paths and carry on downhill into Wasdale Head. The path runs alongside Mosedale Beck, passes the Wasdale packhorse bridge and*

Continued on page 74

comes to the rear of the inn. Turn left to reach the road, then turn right across the front of the inn and continue along the road until the stile is reached which was crossed earlier.

9. ***This stage requires crossing a ford which is liable to flooding in bad weather; if this is the case return to the car park by the road.*** *Take the right hand of the two stiles signposted Public Bridleway and continue straight ahead, through a gate and on to Lingmell Beck which should be forded diagonally heading for the corner of a campsite on the opposite bank. Follow the track through the campsite and just after it turns to the right, cross the fence via a stile and carry on a few more yards to the car park.*

Public Transport
None.

Packhorse bridge, Wasdale Head.

Useful Information

Routes in Order of Difficulty

Easier Walks

Short (up to $3\frac{1}{2}$ miles)
Route 5 – Glenridding & Lanty's Tarn

Medium ($3\frac{1}{2}$ to 5 miles)
Route 9 – High Tilberthwaite & Little Langdale
Route 11 – Keswick Railway & Brundholme Woods
Route 16 – Wasdale Head

Long (over 5 miles)
Route 2 – Claife Heights from Far Sawrey

Moderate Walks

Short (up to $3\frac{1}{2}$ miles)
Route 15 – Stanley Ghyll & the River Esk

Medium ($3\frac{1}{2}$ to 5 miles)
Route 1 – Cat Bells & Brandelhow Park
Route 6 – Gowbarrow Fell & Aira Force
Route 7 – Hallin Fell
Route 10 – Jaws of Borrowdale
Route 12 – Loughrigg Fell & Terrace

Long (over 5 miles)
Route 3 – Dunnerdale Fells & Broughton Mills
Route 4 – Elter Water Round

Harder Walks

Long (over 5 miles)
Route 8 – Hay Stacks & Innominate Tarn
Route 13 – Skiddaw via Ullock Pike
Route 14 – Stickle Tarn, Pavey Ark & Harrison Stickle

Public Transport Operators

(Applicable to the walks)

British Rail	Barrow-in-Furness (0229) 820805
	Carlisle (0228) 44711
Cumberland Motor Services	Whitehaven (0946) 63222
Keswick Launch Co.	Keswick (07687) 72263
Mountain Goat Bus Co.	Windermere (05394) 45161
National Travel (Contact Cumberland or Ribble Motor Services)	
Post Bus (Broughton-in-Furness)	Broughton (0229) 716220
Ravenglass & Eskdale Railway Co.	Ravenglass (0229) 717171
Ribble Motor Services	Lancaster (0524) 64228
Ullswater Navigation & Transit Co.	Kendal (0539) 721626
	Glenridding (07684) 82229
Windermere Vehicle Ferry	Kendal (0539) 20251

National Park Informatio.. Centres

24 hour weather forecast	(05394) 45151
Bowness Bay	(05394) 42895
Coniston	(05394) 41533
Grasmere	(05394) 35245
Hawkshead	(05394) 36525
Keswick	(07687) 72803
Pooley Bridge	(07684) 86530
Seatoller	(07687) 86530
Glenridding	(07684) 82414
Waterhead	(05394) 32729

Wet Weather Alternatives

Museums, Houses, Industrial Archaeology

Brockhole National Park Visitors Centre, Windermere (05394) 46601. Fundamental to an understanding and appreciation of the history, topography, geology and life of the Lake District. April to early November.

Abbot Hall Art Gallery and Museum of Lakeland Life and Industry, Kendal (0539) 722464.

Beatrix Potter Gallery, Hawkeshead (05394) 36355. A collection of her original drawings and well worth seeing. National Trust, April to early November.

Brantwood, near Coniston (05394) 41396. John Ruskin's home and one of the most beautifully situated houses in the Lake District. March to November.

Cumberland Pencil Museum, Keswick (07686) 73626. A fascinating insight into the history of graphite extraction and use in the Borrowdale valley.

Cumberland Toy & Model Museum, Cockermouth (0900) 827606. You can even play with the train set. March to November.

Dove Cottage, Grasmere (05394) 35544. Wordsworth's home during some of his most creative years with permanent and changing exhibitions.

Hill Top, Sawrey (05394) 36269. The home of Beatrix Potter, author of *The Tale of Peter Rabbit* and other children's classics. National Trust, April to early November.

Lakeside & Haverthwaite Railway, near Newby Bridge (05395) 31594. Steam locomotives on display, trains run to Lakeside daily, May to September.

Muncaster Water Mill, near Ravenglass (0229) 717232. Working water-powered corn mill with early 19th century machinery. April to October.

Penrith Steam Museum, Penrith (0768) 62154. Engines on steam most days, Spring Bank Holiday to September.

Stott Park Bobbin Mill, Newby Bridge (05395) 31087. Victorian Mill which is little changed. Telephone for opening hours.

Townend, Troutbeck, near Windermere (05394) 32628. Early 17th century statesman farmer's house full of fascinating domestic implements. National Trust, April to early November.

Tullie House, Carlisle (0228) 34781. The history of border warfare over several centuries.

Wetheriggs Country Pottery, near Penrith (0768) 62946. Mid-19th century pottery and one of the few surviving country potteries producing earthenware. Telephone for opening times.

Windermere Steam Boat Museum, Windermere (05394) 45565. A large collection of steam, motor and sailing boats, Easter to October.

World of Beatrix Potter Exhibition, Bowness (05394) 88444. Open daily, last entrance, 3.30 pm.

Wordsworth House, Cockermouth (0900) 824805. Wordsworth's birthplace, National Trust, April to early November.

Beatrix Potter's home, Hill Top. Sawrey (route 2).

A corner of the garden at Hill Top (note the watering can, rabbits, naughty, for the use of).

Swimming Pools

Appleby-in-Westmorland, Open Air (summer only) (07683) 51212.
Keswick Leisure Pool (07687) 72760.
Penrith (0768) 63450.
Troutbeck, near Windermere (05394) 43243.

Nature Reserves

Asby Scar, near Appleby-in-Westmorland, GR 648103. Nature Conservancy Council, upland grassland and limestone pavement.

Loughrigg Fell Nature Walk, near Ambleside (see Route 12). National Trust, fell and farmland, information from NT Information Centre at the Bridge House by the main car park in Ambleside.

St. Bees Head, near Whitehaven, GR 959118. Royal Society for the Protection of Birds reserve. $2\frac{1}{2}$ mile walk on steep cliffs which are dangerous away from the paths. Herring Gulls, Kittiwakes, Fulmars, occasional Cormorants.

South Walney Nature Reserve, Walney Island off Barrow-in-Furness, GR 215620. Cumbria Trust for Nature Conservation, Immense Gull colonies with other sea-birds, waders, etc. Nature Walks, closed Mondays.

White Moss Common Nature Walk, near Ambleside (see Route 12). National Trust, woodland, fell and farmland. Information from NT Information Centre in Ambleside (see Loughrigg Fell above).

Gardens

Acorn Bank, Temple Sowerby, near Penrith (07683) 61281. National Trust, excellent walled herb garden, April to early November.

Lingholm Gardens, Portinscale, near Keswick (07687) 72003. Formal and woodland gardens.

Rydal Mount, near Ambleside (05394) 33002. National Trust, once Wordsworth's home and possessed of one of the most interesting small gardens in England.

Sizergh Castle, near Kendal (05395) 60070. National Trust, contains the NT's largest rock garden, April to early November.

There are more sheep than people in the Lake District.

Woodland and Forest Trails

Dodd Wood, Mirehouse, near Keswick (07687) 76616. Forestry Commission, several graded and waymarked walks.

Grizedale Forest Park, near Hawkeshead (0229) 860373. Forestry Commission, several graded and waymarked walks, FC shop and information centre is open from Easter to October only but the sculpture trail map is usually available from the local pub.

Whinlatter Visitor Centre, Whinlatter Pass, near Keswick (07687) 78469. Forestry Commission, forest and geology trails, permanent orienteering courses, exhibition.

Country Parks

Appleby Castle Conservation Centre, Appleby-in-Westmorland (07683) 51402. Rare Breeds Survival Trust Centre, Easter to September.

Fell Foot Park, Newby Bridge (05395) 71273. National Trust, 18 acre country park with lakeshore access.

Lowther Leisure Park, near Penrith (09312) 523. Excellent adventure playground with numerous rides and a circus. Easter week, Spring Bank Holiday to early September, telephone for further details.

Mirehouse, near Keswick (07687) 72287. Wood and lakeside walks, 2 adventure playgrounds, graded by age.

Take the 'Ratty' to the starting point of route 15.

THE FAMILY WALKS SERIES

Family Walks on Anglesey. Laurence Main. ISBN 0 907758 665.
Family Walks in Berkshire & North Hampshire. Kathy Sharp. ISBN 0 907758 371.
Family Walks around Bristol, Bath & the Mendips. Nigel Vile. ISBN 0 907758 193.
Family Walks around Cardiff & the Valleys. Gordon Hindess. ISBN 0 907758 541.
Family Walks in Cheshire. Chris Buckland. ISBN 0 907758 290.
Family Walks in Cornwall. John Caswell. ISBN 0 907758 55X.
Family Walks in the Cotswolds. Gordon Ottewell. ISBN 0 907758 150.
Family Walks on Exmoor & the Quantocks. John Caswell. ISBN 0 907758 460.
Family Walks in South Gloucestershire. Gordon Ottewell. ISBN 0 907758 339.
Family Walks in Gower. Amanda Green. ISBN 0 907758 630.
Family Walks in Hereford and Worcester. Gordon Ottewell. ISBN 0 907758 207.
Family Walks on the Isle of Wight. Laurence Main. ISBN 0 907758 568.
Family Walks in North West Kent. Clive Cutter. ISBN 0 907758 363.
Family Walks in the Lake District. Barry McKay. ISBN 0 907758 401.
Family Walks in Mendip, Avalon & Sedgemoor. Nigel Vile. ISBN 0 907758 41X.
Family Walks in the New Forest. Nigel Vile. ISBN 0 907758 606.
Family Walks in Oxfordshire. Laurence Main. ISBN 0 907758 38X.
Family Walks in the Dark Peak. Norman Taylor. ISBN 0 907758 169.
Family Walks in the White Peak. Norman Taylor. ISBN 0 907758 096.
Family Walks in South Derbyshire. Gordon Ottewell. ISBN 0 907758 614.
Family Walks in South Shropshire. Marian Newton. ISBN 0 907758 304.
Family Walks in Snowdonia. Laurence Main. ISBN 0 907758 320.
Family Walks in the Staffordshire Peaks and Potteries. Les Lumsdon. ISBN 0 907758 347.
Family Walks around Stratford & Banbury. Gordon Ottewell. ISBN 0 907758 495.
Family Walks in Suffolk. C J Francis. ISBN 0 907758 649.
Family Walks around Swansea. Raymond Humphreys. ISBN 0 907758 622.
Family Walks in the Teme Valley. Camilla Harrison. ISBN 0 907758 452.
Family Walks in Three Peaks & Malham. Howard Beck. ISBN 0 907758 428
Family Walks in Mid Wales. Laurence Main. ISBN 0 907758 274.
Family Walks in the North Wales Borderlands. Gordon Emery. ISBN 0 907758 509.
Family Walks in Warwickshire. Geoff Allen. ISBN 0 907758 533.
Family Walks in the Weald of Kent & Sussex. Clive Cutter. ISBN 0 907758 517.
Family Walks in Wiltshire. Nigel Vile. ISBN 0 907758 215.
Family Walks in the Wye Valley. Heather & Jon Hurley. ISBN 0 907758 266.
Family Walks in the North Yorkshire Dales. Howard Beck. ISBN 0 907758 525.
Family Walks in South Yorkshire. Norman Taylor. ISBN 0 907758 258.
Family Walks in West Yorkshire. Howard Beck. ISBN 0 907758 436.

The publishers welcome suggestions for further titles in this series; and will be pleased to consider manuscripts relating to Derbyshire from new or established authors.

Scarthin Books of Cromford, in the Peak District, are also leading second-hand and antiquarian booksellers, and are eager to purchase specialised material, both ancient and modern.
Contact Dr D. J. Mitchell, 0629-823272.